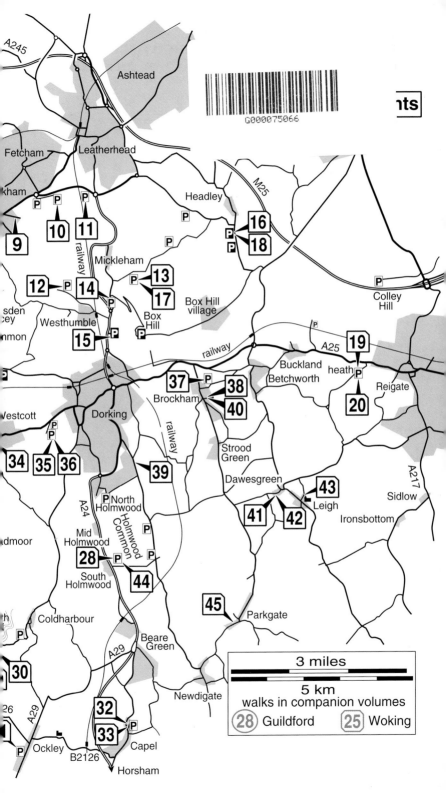

1 Sheepleas and the Lovelace Arches

About 9 km/5½ miles with a short cut of 1½km/1 mile; forest and farmland, steep slopes, bluebells. OS maps 1:25000 145 +146, 1:50000 187 Dorking.

Start at Shere Road Sheepleas car park, TQ 084 514. Green Dene Sheepleas car park, TQ 091 509, is near the route

Linking walks
2◇ 3◆ ⑰✳ ㊳✴

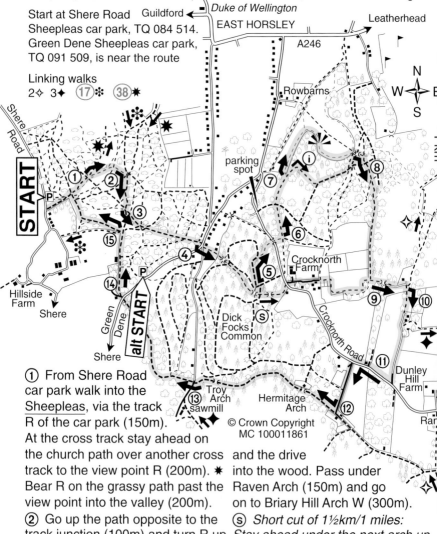

© Crown Copyright MC 100011861

① From Shere Road car park walk into the Sheepleas, via the track R of the car park (150m). At the cross track stay ahead on the church path over another cross track to the view point R (200m). ✳ Bear R on the grassy path past the view point into the valley (200m).
② Go up the path opposite to the track junction (100m) and turn R up the main (& steepest) track to the oblique crossing bridleway (250m).
③ Bear L up this. At the junction on top (150m), stay ahead down through the trees into Green Dene (400m). Cross the road to the lane.
④ Just into the lane, take the bridleway up L between the field

and the drive into the wood. Pass under Raven Arch (150m) and go on to Briary Hill Arch W (300m).
Ⓢ *Short cut of 1½km/1 miles: Stay ahead under the next arch up to the road (250m), along the drive of Crocknorth Farm opposite, past houses (250m) then on the path between fields (80m). Now make for the forest at the far side of the fields: Go round the R edge of the fields to the path junction at the corner of the forest (400m).* ◆⑨

2

⑤ Just after the arch (and 60m before the next arch) go L on the track (50m) then L & R (20m) and along the brow of the hill (200m) until round the R bend (40m). On the L bend take the path R to the road cutting (150m). Cross the Dorking (Lovelace) Bridge and go on to the next cross path (50m).

⑥ Turn L down the slope (200m) Cross the forest track (100m from the road and parking spot L). Keep on down into the dry valley and up. Watch out for the path L before the corner of a field visible through the trees (200m).

⑦ The best route is in the field but there is no public right of way and the path may get closed. Turn L into the field. Follow the path up the R edge to the corner of the wood (300m), round R still near the wood (Horsley Towers is visible looking back), to the public path in dip (400m). Turn R into the wood to Stony Dene Arch. ➔⑧

ⓘ *If the field path is closed, carry on up round the R bend and across the top of the hill to a major forest track (250m). Turn L down this track (200m). Between slight L & R bends at the bottom turn L on the cross path near the field to Stoney Dene Arch (100m).*

⑧ Take the path away from the field under the arch to the cross path (50m) and turn R up the slight slope. Stay ahead over the top (500m) and ahead beside fields to the corner of the forest L (350m).

⑨ Follow the path away from the corner of the field along the end of the forest and under Meadow Plat Arch to the tarmac drive (120m). Descend past the house (120m). ✧

⑩ Turn R on the path at the edge of the wood (200m). Stay ahead past two houses on the tarmac drive, ✦ over the rise and down to Crocknorth Road (450m).

⑪ Walk along the road R past the wood into the dip with a house R (200m) and up to the forest track L (100m). Follow the forest track to the T-junction near a house (350m).

⑫ Turn R on the byway through the forest. Keep to the track down under Hermitage Arch (300m) and Troy Arch (650m) to the tarmac at Honeysuckle Bottom near the sawmill (150m).

⑬ Stay ahead up the steep path opposite, round a R curve and down to Green Dene (road) (800m)

⑭ Continue ahead up the path opposite, over the hill and on beside the field L (450m). ✳

⑮ Just after the field turn L down the track (300m). Pass round the R bend (200m) and take the next L to the car park (150m).

The **Lovelace Arches** were built in the 1860s for William King, 1st Earl Lovelace, it is said, for forestry carts to cross existing byways. There were 15 arches initiall but only ten survive, being restored in recent times. Their arches are usually horseshoe shaped with brick and flint masonry, but in a great variety of sizes, 6-18' wide.

Earl Lovelace owned East Horsley and Ockham manors where flint and ornate brickwork are a feature of the estate buildings. He lived at theGothic mansion, HorsleyTowers. Originally called East Horsley Park, it was built by Sir Charles Barry for William Currie. Earl Lovelace enlarged it and added the towers in the 1830s. Ada, Lady Lovelace was Byron's daughter. Tommy Sopwith later lived there.

2 Ranmore Manor and Yewtree Farm

About 6¾ km/4¼ miles with an extension of 2½ km/1½ miles to White Down. Farmland and woods. OS maps 1:25000 146 Dorking, 1:50000 187 Dorking.

Start from Stony Rock car park, Hogden Lane, TQ 124 504, or, on the extension, from White Downs car park, TQ 114 494.

Linking walks
1✧ 3✪ 7☆
8✳ 22✳

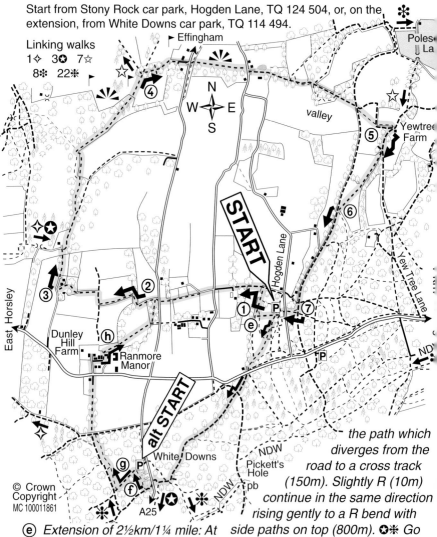

(e) *Extension of 2½km/1¼ mile: At Stony Rock car park take the path away from the road briefly (40m from parking area) and turn along the 2nd side path L (70m). At the 1st cross path, diverge R and stay ahead to the road at the SW corner of Ranmore Common near a house (450m). Opposite the house, take*

the path which diverges from the road to a cross track (150m). Slightly R (10m) continue in the same direction rising gently to a R bend with side paths on top (800m). ✪✳ *Go round the bend and down to the road (100m). Slightly L walk up the forest track on the other side (80m).* (f) *Watch out for a side path R and follow it to the car park (150m).* (g) *From the top of White Downs car park follow the uphill path away from the road (200m). Just before*

4

the cross track turn R on the path parallel with the track down to the bottom edge of the forest (400m).✧ Opposite the end of the track follow the path between fields (400m). Continue over the road along the drive of Dunley Hill Farm (100m).

ⓗ *Turn R on the side track beside the buildings (60m) then L between buildings to the fields (60m). In the field turn R but diverge from the R edge to the corner near the trees (100m). Continue over the next field in the same line to the corner of the wood (250m). In the wood bear L on the side path diagonally to the bottom (200m).* ➔②

① From Stony Rock car park take the path away from the road (200m) and turn R along the field hedge to the corner (200m). Exit L then stay ahead: between fields (200m), down a house drive (100m), over a road, up a house drive to the bend (100m), along the R edge of the fields (200m) and down to the road (100m) opposite a path.

② Go up the R edge of the wood (80m) and on along the R edge of the field to a belt of trees R (60m). Turn R through the trees to the hedge L (80m) and follow it to the farm track (250m). Walk along the track R (100m) and enter the end of the L field. Go along the R edge to the corner of the wood (100m). Descend through the wood towards the house and go L beside the garden to the drive (200m).

③ Turn R on the drive past the houses and carry on along the path between fields to the next house (300m). At the drive turn R on the path through the wood to the fork (300m). Follow the L footpath up

into a field (250m). Walk up round the L edge to the next corner (150m). Re-enter the wood and turn R along the path outside the field, eventually emerging at the top of the golf course (500m). Cross the fairway slightly R to the clump of trees (120m). Take the path into the clump, 40m from the L end, to the cross path (20m). ☆

④ Turn R. Go along the clump, over a golf track, to the end (100m). Cross the next fairway slightly L to the path at the end of the large trees (100m). Stay ahead beside the garden (60m) and along the track to the road (100m). Opposite, go through the trees and on along the top edge of the field (400m). Cross the next road slightly R (20m) and continue on the broad horse track between the gardens. ✳ Keep on between fields and woods (500m) and descend steeply into a dry valley (300m). Slightly R (30m) enter the field corner between the tracks and ascend obliquely to the hedge-end (100m). Cross the track into the next field and follow the R edge to the track junction (100m).

⑤ Outside, at Yewtree Farm, go R on the track to the L curve (200m) and into the corner of the hillside field R. Follow the top edge until it bends L (250m) then descend obliquely (towards distant houses) to the bottom corner (200m).

⑥ Walk up the valley track L, past the end of the lane from houses above R (300m) and near 2 houses R (400m). Disregard the cross path at the end of the garden and carry on to the next cross path (40m).

⑦ Turn R up to Hogden Lane opposite the car park (50m).

3 White Downs and Dick Focks Common

About 9½km/6 miles; forest and chalk grassland; short steep slopes; grand views. OS maps 1:25000 145 +146, 1:50000 187 Dorking.

Start at Stony Rock car park, Hogden Lane, at the western edge of Ranmore Common, TQ 124 504. White Downs car park is close to the route, TQ 114 494.

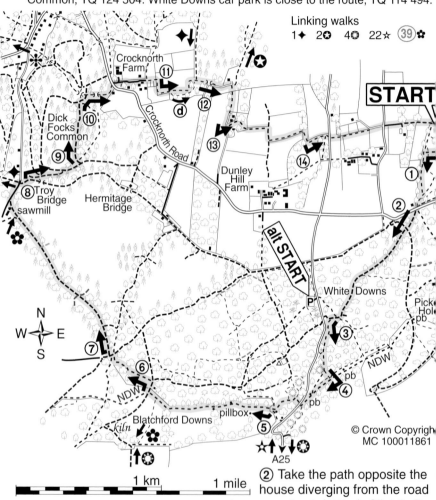

Linking walks

1✦   2✿   4✿   22★   ㉟ ✿

© Crown Copyright
MC 100011861

② Take the path opposite the house diverging from the road to a cross track (150m). Slightly R (10m) continue on the track in the same direction, rising gently to a R bend with side paths on top (800m).

③ Go round the bend and down (60m). At the next R bend diverge on the side path L. The path bends several times near the road. Carry on to the chalk pit R (350m).

① At Stony Rock car park take the path directly away from the road to the boundary path of Ranmore Common, outside fields (150m). Turn L along the boundary path and stay ahead to the road at the SW corner of the common, near a house (350m).★

④ Fork L down to the path on the brow of the hill (60m). Turn R along the brow, passing a <u>pillbox</u>, to the road (200m). ✪ Slightly R cross the road and ascend the steep path opposite (NDW)(50m). Go round a L bend on top and down to a cross path near the next pillbox (200m).

⑤ Stay on the path ahead just below the brow of the <u>North Downs</u>, gently undulating past more pill boxes and, eventually rising to a cross track (900m). ✿

⑥ Turn R over the top into the trees (100m) then L at the staggered cross path to the major forest track (300m).

⑦ Don't take the path almost opposite but turn L on the forest track (30m) then R down the next side track. Stay ahead downhill to the sawmill drive in the valley (Honeysuckle Bottom) (1200m) and bear R on it to the tarmac road (100m). ✦

⑧ At the start of the road take the byway R (100m). From the bend before Troy (Lovelace) Arch cross to the parallel track L (20m). Follow it ahead steeply up the hill of Dick Focks Common (200m). On top stay ahead on the level track R to the next side track back L (120m)

⑨ Turn L on this track. Eventually pass round a R bend at side tracks (400m) then a L bend to a sloping cross path (80m) with Lovelace arches down L and up R.

⑩ Turn R up under the arch (60m) and keep on to the road (250m). Go along Crocknorth Farm drive opposite (250m). After the houses stay ahead between fields (80m). At the large field identify the forest with pines on the far side.

⑪ Skirt round the R edge to the corner of the pines (400m).

ⓓ *At bluebell time digress via the path in the belt of trees R of the large field (400m).*

⑫ At the cross path on the corner of the forest, walk away from the field along the edge of the forest. Go under Meadow Plat Arch to the drive (120m) and down past a house L (120m). ✪ Turn R on the path at the edge of the wood and stay ahead past houses (300m).

⑬ Turn L on the footpath after the 2nd house. Follow it up through the trees round R to the field (150m). Go L along the edge (150m), R on the farm track (100m) and L along the hedge at the end of the field (200m). In the belt of trees turn R and enter the next field (80m).

⑭ Turn L along the edge then stay ahead: into the valleyside wood (60m), down to the road (80m), up the field opposite past the end of the thicket (50m), along the fence (200m) and drive (100m), over the road, down the drive (100m), up between fields to Ranmore Common (200m) and on to the house at the road (150m). Turn R to the car park (100m).

The Forestry Commission has an open access policy for walkers but sections have to be closed temporarily for logging operations. Small paths suddenly become deep-rutted tracks which after a few years fade away. The Commission was set up in 1919, after World War I, for the strategic supply of timber. It provides policy, advice and grants and has research and commercial divisions, the latter being responsible for educational and recreational uses which includes the provision of footpaths and horse rides.

4 Abinger Common and the North Downs

About 9½ km/6 miles with a short cut of 2½ km/1½ miles; hilly farmland; long views; one steep climb. OS maps 1:25000 146 Dorking 1:50000 187 Dorking.

Start at Abinger Roughs car park, TQ 111 480, or Abinger Church, TQ 115 459.

Linking walks 3❂ 21★
22✳ (24)✳ (39)✳ (40)☆

The Abinger Hatch ☎ 01306 730737
The Volunteer ☎ 01306 730798

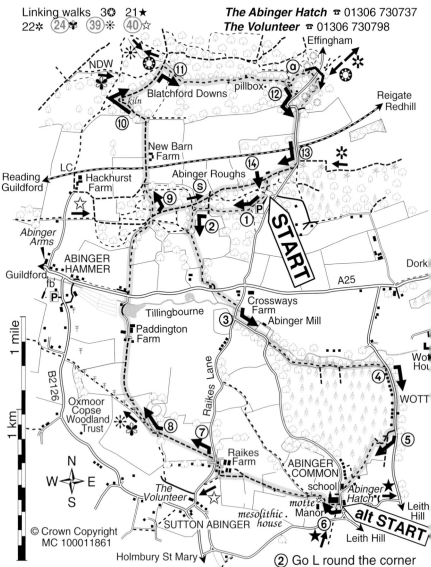

① In the Roughs car park, facing away from the road, take the path L: round a R curve, down near a field to a cleft in the ridge (450m), up to the corner of the field (50m).

② Go L round the corner and on above the field (150m). Just round the R bend turn L to the field and go straight down to the lowest point (250m). Carry on between gardens to the main road (200m).

8

③ Cross into the field and follow the oblique path L to the next road (200m). Go R (100m) then L along Abinger Lane past the house, Abinger Mill (300m). At the R bend stay ahead on the path near the Tillingbourne, eventually curving R up to the road (800m).

④ Walk up the road R past the Wotton estate cottages (400m)

⑤ After the last house turn R on the track which bends L & R (50m). When it branches take the middle track which soon curves R up into the trees. Carry on up the path round the pine plantation and L of the school to the road in Abinger Common village (600m). Turn L to the ***Abinger Hatch*** (50m). ★

⑥ Enter the main church gate and carry on out at the back of the churchyard towards Abinger Manor and R round the S-bend past the motte L (200m). Disregard the side path diverging R downhill (100m) and carry on between fields (450m). Fork L before Raikes Farm outside the farmyard (200m). ☆

⑦ Go round the R bend, between houses to the farmyard. Opposite the barns exit L to the road (80m). Slightly R (20m) turn L into the first field. Follow the diagonal track across the field (400m).

⑧ In the next field bear R on the path between the fields. Disregard the diverging side path L (100m) ✳✿ and descend to Paddington Farm (600m). Slightly L, continue ahead down the drive, winding between a millpond R and the large Abinger Hammer Mill Pond L (watercress) to the road (300m). Cross and go up the sunken path (200m) then the L edge to the next gate (300m) and out to the cross track in Abinger Roughs (70m).

Ⓢ *Short cut of 2½ km/1½ mile: Bear R on the main track obliquely across the clearing to the 1st field L (350m). Stay on this track near the fields down to a shed L (500m).* ➔⑭

⑨ Bear R briefly on the main track (40m) then take the path L out of the corner of the clearing and down through the trees to the farm track between fields (250m). Follow the track R, over the railway, past New Barn Farm and ahead between fields (400m).

⑩ At the North Downs escarpment follow the L bend and ascend in trees (250m). At the junction (and lime kiln) turn R up the track until out of the trees (400m). ✪

⑪ Just before the thicket on top take the path R across the field descending initially then undulating along the hillside just below the trees. Pass two pillboxes close to the path and a third, 30m below it and keep on to the cross path just before the 4th pillbox (700m). ✳

Ⓐ *Adventurous route: Go on over the rise and round a R bend down to the road (200m). Just into the path on the other side (5m) (not at the edge) take the path R, soon dropping steeply, L of chalk pits, to the cart track and road (250m).* ➔⑬

⑫ Turn down the steep path R to the road (100m). Go down the road round the steep S bend (200m).

⑬ Walk down over the railway (250m). After the bridge (100m) take the first path R into Abinger Roughs, to the barn R (200m).

⑭ Turn up the side path beside the Wilberforce Memorial over the rise to the car park (100m).

5 Great Ridings Wood and Effingham Common

About 8½ km/5¼ miles. A short cut of 1 km/¾ mile and extension of 1 km/¾ mile can be used together. A mainly level London Clay walk through woods and farmland; summer shade. OS maps 1:25000 146 Dorking, 1:50000 187 Dorking.

Start from the Effingham sports club car park off Browns Lane, TQ 119 534. If linking to Walk 51 start from the kerbside in Orestan Road, TQ 108 535, or from Effingham Common car park at the cricket ground, TQ 105 552.

Linking walks 6❋ 7☆

The Sir Douglas Haig 01372 456886
The Plough ☎ 01372 458121

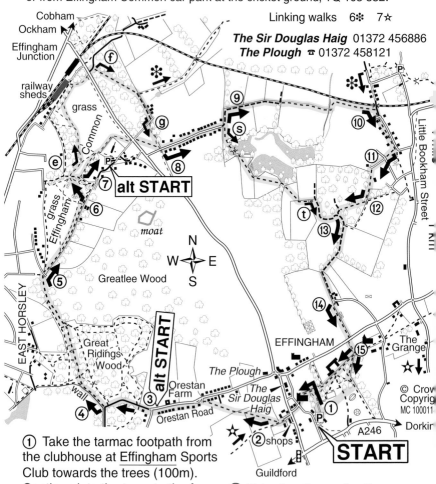

© Crow
Copyrig
MC 100011

① Take the tarmac footpath from the clubhouse at Effingham Sports Club towards the trees (100m). Continue into the trees to the far edge (100m) then turn L (100m). Cross the churchyard to the far L corner (50m) and go down the little road opposite to the village street (100m). Cross slightly L and take the drive past the end of the shops. Keep on to the first field R (100m).

② Take the diagonal path across the field (250m). Continue obliquely eventually joining the road (300m). Go L along the pavement (350m).
③ From the end of Orestan Road take the track into the wood. Stay on the track over the rise to the junction at flint walls (350m).

10

④ Turn R down the track beside the wall (300m). Stay ahead on the path across Great Ridings Wood to the road with houses (800m).

⑤ Cross the road into Effingham Common. Follow the R edge past a house R (450m) & stables (100m).

⑥ After the stables bear L across the grass passing R of the two clumps of trees and out through the line of trees (200m). ❊ Turn R.

ⓔ *Extension of 1 km/¾ mile: Follow paths around the L edge of the grass near the fringe of trees, all the way to the road (near Effingham Junction) (700m).*

ⓕ *Go down the drive on the other side (50m) and take the side path R through the wood (400m). Bear R along the track outside the wood past the farm buildings (300m).*

ⓖ *Follow the drive out R to the Common (40m) and take the path L along the edge (150m).* ➧⑧

⑦ Follow paths along the line of trees fringing the R edge of the grass (250m). Carry on round the cricket field to the drive (300m). Cross the road to the farm drive opposite but take the oblique path R over the grass (200m).

⑧ Turn along the road L to the far end (450m) and go into the field.

ⓢ *Short cut of 1 km/¾ mile: Walk down the R edge (80m) and cross the corner to the gate (80m). Go out, over the bridge and over the drive to the next field (80m). Cross the L corner and follow the L edge (200m). At the corner of the pond fence, bear L in a straight line across the curve to the gate at the L corner (200m). Pass the pond into the next field (40m) and cross diagonally to the top corner (150m).*

ⓣ *In the field above turn L along the fence to the track (100m) then R on track outside the fields. Stay on the same track round L & R curves (300m) and on.* ➧⑬

⑨ Follow the cart track L, round the corner R (100m) and on until it bends L (400m). Stay ahead through the fields near the L hedge and ditch (350m). In the field before the farm, cross to the L edge over the footbridge (50m). Follow the railway fence up R to the track from the railway bridge (300m).

⑩ Turn R (50m). Cross the road and follow the path R of it (250m).

⑪ Just before the road bends L, take the path R between gardens (100m). Cross a road and follow the drive opposite (100m). When it bends into the end garden, turn L along the path between gardens to the first field L (200m)

⑫ At the cross path from the field turn R through the wood (200m) and L at the end out to fields (30m). Turn L on the track.

⑬ Follow the curving track past the end of the wood (100m) and stay on it between fields all the way down to houses (600m).

⑭ At the junction of drives with the tarmac road look for the path R between hedges. Go out to the field (50m) and follow the L edge to the road (250m), Cross slightly R (20m) and continue to the cross path between the school R and Little Bookham Church L (100m).✫ Turn R.

⑮ If making for the sports club take any side path L through the trees and cross R (500m). If not stay ahead past the school to the churchyard (450m).

6 Bookham and Effingham Commons

About 9 km/5½ miles with a short cut of 2½ km/1¾ miles; farmland and woods on the London Clay, gently undulating. OS maps 1:25000 146 Dorking, 1:50000 187 Dorking.

Start at Bookham Common Plains car park (NT/free), TQ 125 558. There are are also free NT car parks at Hundred Pound Bridge TQ 120 567 and Mark Oak, TQ 133 568. Near the route is Effingham Common car park, TQ 105 552.

Linking walk 5❈

The Windsor Castle 01372 452226

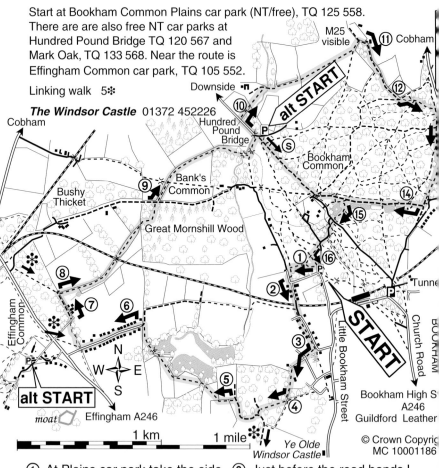

① At Plains car park take the side path L immediately after the cattle grid, winding around the trees, into the SW corner of Bookham Common (200m). At the T-junction turn L & R to the lane (50m).

② Walk L along the lane (40m). When it bends L take the smaller lane ahead and keep on over the railway to the next road (250m). Cross and follow the footpath ahead R of the road (250m).

③ Just before the road bends L, take the path R between gardens (100m). Cross a road and follow the drive opposite (100m). When it bends into the end garden, turn L along the path between gardens to the first field L (200m).

④ At the cross path from the field turn R across the wood (200m) and L, at the end, to the fields (30m). ❈ Follow the track R winding round the edge of the wood (250m).

12

⑤ When the track enters the field follow the path L outside the fence (100m) and turn R into the corner of the 2nd adjacent field. Cross diagonally to the corner at the wood (150m) and go through the trees past the corner of the pond to the next field (50m). Cut across the curve of the R edge to the end of the trees (200m) then follow the R edge and go straight on over to the L corner (200m). Outside the field, cross the farm drive and the pond dam up to the next field (80m). Ascend across the L corner and go up the L edge to the road (150m).

⑥ Follow the road (450m). After the houses turn R along the edge of Effingham Common (200m).

⑦ Follow the farm drive away from the green briefly (40m) then turn L on the path along the edge of the wood past the farm buildings to the first field R (200m).

⑧ Take the path R between hedges (150m). Go on along the narrow field (350m), under the railway, between fields (300m) then through the wood round a L bend (100m) to the track (100m).

⑨ Slightly R (20m), take the path on the other side, between fields to the end of the R field (500m), then through scrub and over a footbridge to a path junction (250m). Turn L over the footbridge to Hundred Pound Bridge and car park (150m).

Ⓢ *Short cut of 2½ km/1¾ miles: From Hundred Pound Bridge, before the car park, take the wide 2nd side path R. Keep on to the junction near buildings (600m). Stay on the same path round a slight L bend (150m). At the next cross path turn R to the pond.* ➔⑮

⑩ Walk along the road to the end of the wood (100m) and take the path R down the edge of the field (100m). Stay ahead converging on the stream (200m). Cross the farm bridge and go straight up past hedge end L. Carry on up the L edge and through the hedge on the ridge top (250m). Cross the great field towards the clump of trees seen R of the house (400m). At the edge turn L into the corner (80m).

⑪ Outside the field follow the horse track R (50m), round a R bend and down the edge of the Bookham Common trees to the T-junction after the fields (400m).

⑫ Turn L outside the field (20m) and take the path up R cutting the corner to the next path from the direction of the field (80m). Follow this path R past a pond L (60m) to the cross track just before Mark Oak car park (100m). Turn R.

⑬ Follow the horse track in the trees past paths from Mark Oak car park, over a staggered cross track (100m), and down to a fork (100m). Fork L down the footpath, soon in a long narrow glade, to the track (350m). Continue ahead (R) (50m).

⑭ Turn R on the wide path. Pass ponds L, causeway path L (300m) then more ponds (350m). At the next cross path turn L to the pond.

⑮ Follow the broad path L round the pond to the vehicle track behind it (200m). Cross the track and go along the path to the next track (40m). Follow that L, out of the trees, to the track junction (150m).

⑯ Cross the bridge then take the footpath diverging R of the track (100m). At the cross path turn L to Plains car park (100m).

7 Effingham and Polesden Lacey

About 9km/5½ miles with a 2km/1½ miles extension around PolesdenLacey.
Undulating farm country on the north face of the North Downs. Polesden Lacey
(NT) can be visited. OS maps 1:25000 146 Dorking 1:50000 187 Dorking.

Start from the Effingham sports field car park off Browns Lane, TQ 119 534.
At Polesden Lacey start from the North Lodge (free) car park, TQ 135 527.

Linking walks 2☆ 5★ 8★ 9✿

The Sir Douglas Haig 01372 456886
The Plough 01372 458121

★① At the Effingham sports fields
cross the grass to the corner at the
trees furthest from the A246
(300m). Turn L along the path at
the edge and stay on it when it
bends ½R along the fence (200m).
② Bear R on the path from the
school passing R of Little <u>Bookham</u>
Church to the road (250m). Stay
ahead to the next road (300m).
③ Walk up the road R (Rectory
Lane) to the main road (700m).
④ Cross slightly R and walk up
Chalkpit Lane, a track. Keep on to

open fields L but watch out for the
hedge crossing towards the distant
Goldstone Farm L (750m).
⑤ Just after it (10m) enter the field.
Identify the top edge and cross
obliquely to the L corner (350m).☆
⑥ Outside, follow the track L
(300m). ✿ Continue on the farm
drive briefly then cut across the
parking area R and the grass to
the lodge and main drive (100m).

14

⑦ Walk along the fence R or L of the drive almost to the main gates of <u>Polesden Lacey</u> (350m).

ⓔ *Extension of 2km/1½ miles around Polesden Lacey: Turn L into the field and follow the R edge (250m). Go round the R bend then diverge from the R edge to the far L corner (200m). Go through gates to the next field (30m) and cross ½L to the gate (200m).*

ⓕ *In the wood turn R immediately on the path near the edge (250m). At the drive cross into the field opposite and descend steeply to the bottom L corner (250m). ★*

ⓖ *In the next field turn R along the edge (350m). Stay ahead: wood, field, wood, field (450m). Just before the farm, turn R into the trees and follow the path to the tarmac drive (150m). Walk up under the garden bridges (400m). Turn L at the field. ➜⑨*

⑧ Go R through the NT car park to the far L corner (300m). Outside the car park go round the bend past the house (50m) and turn R.

⑨ Follow the track at the edge of the field (200m). Just round the corner turn L across the track in the trees and carry on between fields. Go round the S-bend (200m) but not round the next bend R (150m). There are two side paths ahead. Take the R one just round the bend, through trees and over the field obliquely to the corner (450m).

⑩ Turn R on the track outside the field and stay on it to the road

(300m). Cross into the field slightly R. Follow the top edge (350m) then bear L through the trees to the next road (30m). Cross to the drive opposite and follow the track from it continuing on the path to the golf course (150m). Bear L across the fairway to the path in the clump of trees (100m). Follow the path in the trees. After the 2nd cross path curve R to the edge (150m).

⑪ Follow the right-of-way down the slope of the golf course 30m L of the hedge end. Diverge from the hedge towards the distant tele-communication towers and skirt R of the small clump of trees (200m). Continue in the same line down through the hedge (100m), across the hedge corner with house below (150m) and over the grass to the shed in the trees (200m). Follow the path L to the road and cross to the pavement (100m)

⑫ Turn R (20m) then L & R on the path behind the trees (100m). Follow the unmade Salmons Road L down to the lowest point (350m). Before the last house enter the corner of the L field and, diverging from the R edge, cross to the middle of the top edge at the R end of the clump of trees (250m). Go on between fields (600m) then along the drive to the Street in <u>Effingham</u> (100m) (down the road L is the ***Sir Douglas Haig*** 200m). Slightly L, go up the road opposite to the churchyard (150m). Pass round the church and out at the far L corner near the flint wall (100m).

⑬ In the trees behind the church yard, turn R on one of the side paths to the sports field and cross ahead to the car park (200m).

West-humble

Connicut Lane

ⓕ

Tanner's Hatch ⓖ

8 Polesden Lacey and Ranmore Common

About 8 km/5 miles with an extension of 1 km/¾ mile. A North Downs walk; woods, chalk grassland and the Polesden Lacey park. The house (NT) can be visited. OS maps 1:25000 146 Dorking, 1:50000 187 Dorking.

Start at North Lodge (NT/free) car park near Polesden Lacey, TQ 135 527, or at Polesden Lacey itself or at the Denbies Hillside car park (NT/pay), TQ 142 153, or, on the extension, at Ranmore Common car park, TQ 126 502 (NT/free).

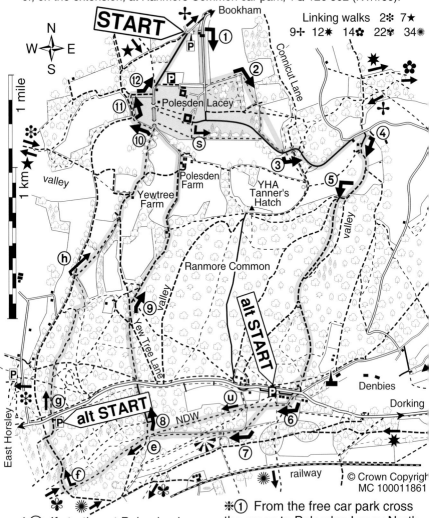

Linking walks 2✳ 7★ 9✛ 12✳ 14✿ 22✳ 34✳

© Crown Copyright MC 100011861

✛Ⓢ *If starting at Polesden Lacey itself, make your way to the house then cross the lawn to the bottom hedge. Follow the hedge L to join the carriage way (500m) and stay ahead down it (200m).* ✛③

✳① From the free car park cross the grass to Polesden Lacey North Lodge (50m) and go along the drive or verge almost to the gate (350m).
② Turn L into the field and follow the R edge (250m). Go R round the corner but diverge from the R edge

to the far L corner (200m). Pass through gates and over a track to the next field (30m). ✳ Make for the bottom L corner either round the R hedge (400m) or directly (300m). Outside the gate turn L on the old carriage way.

③ Continue over the bridge (70m), all the way down to the lodge and road (500m). Walk down the road to the first side track R (100m).

④ Follow the track round to the farm buildings and carry on up between fields towards the wood (250m). Disregard the L fork and keep on across the field into the wood (Ranmore Common) (200m).

⑤ Disregard a side track L (70m) but soon after it (30m) turn L and avoid branch tracks R. Keep on up through the Common to the fork (750m). Fork L then stay ahead to the top edge of the wood near a house (possibly hidden by trees) (600m). Go round R of the house to the road junction (50m).

⑥ Opposite the side road cross into the field at Denbies Hillside (NDW)(50m) and follow the garden hedge to the bend (70m). ✲✳ Turn R past the next hedge bend (50m) to the oblique cross track (100m).

ⓤ *If you need shade stay ahead on the NDW into the wood (120m) and through it to the cross path after the field L (700m).* ➜⑧ *or* ➜ⓔ

⑦ Bear L on the oblique crosspath to the corner of the wood over the brow of the hill (200m) then follow the bottom edge of the wood up to the top R corner of the field (650m). Outside, go L to the junction (30m).

ⓔ *Extension of 1km/¾ mile: Continue on the North Downs Way to the next cross track (600m).*

ⓕ *Turn R up through the forestry plantation. Stay on this track past cross tracks and round bends to the road at Ranmore Common Car Park (500m).*

ⓖ *From the car park exit, cross the road and follow the horse track opposite through the trees (350m) over a major cross track ✤ and on until it bends L (400m). Take the little path R down to the valley path (50m) and descend L to the stoney track (200m). ★*

ⓗ *In the next field R, ascend obliquely aiming for the top corner (200m). Go on along the edge to the next corner (250m) then along the track L (150m) past Yew Tree Farm down to the fork (150m). Go L into the valley and up to the bend in the tarmac drive (300m).* ➜⑩

⑧ Take the track R to the road (350m). Continue on the path opposite directly away from the road. Disregard cross paths and eventually join the vehicle track converging R (400m).

⑨ A bit further on (100m) take the next side track, diverging R. Stay ahead past a house and into a field (600m). Carry on down the R edge, past Polesden Farm R (500m) and up the tarmac drive to the R bend before the garden bridge (250m).

⑩ Take the path L up the R edge of the field (200m). ★

⑪ At the track turn R and take the path R of the track outside the Polesden Lacey garden up to the next track (150m). ✢

⑫ Turn R along the edge of the field to the tarmac drive (150m) then L (50m). Either turn R into the NT car park or continue ahead to the free car park (400m).

9 Bookham, Chapel Farm and Polesden Lacey

About 9km/5¾ miles with a short cut of 2km/1¼ miles. Farmland and woods on the North Downs; undulating. Good in winter; bluebells in season.
OS maps 1:25000 146 Dorking, 1:50000 187 Dorking.

Start from the kerbside at the top of Downs Way in Bookham, TQ 145 543.
The Fetcham car park on the A246, TQ 151 549, and Crabtree Lane
car park, TQ 158 524, near Westhumble are near
the route as are the Polesden Lacey car parks.

Linking walks 7✿ 8✛ 10★ 11❀ 12✦

Polesden Lacey ☎ 01372 452048.
Tea Room ☎ 01372 456190

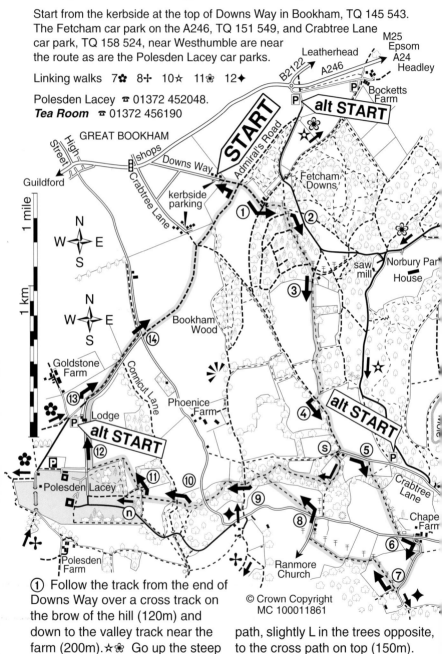

① Follow the track from the end of
Downs Way over a cross track on
the brow of the hill (120m) and
down to the valley track near the
farm (200m).★❀ Go up the steep

© Crown Copyright
MC 100011861

path, slightly L in the trees opposite,
to the cross path on top (150m).

18

② Turn R along the ridge path which eventually curves down L to a complex junction of tracks and house drives (450m).

③ Turn R up the valley track soon ending at fields (100m). Continue ahead on the permissive path at the R edge of the L field (150m). Keep on through the wood on paths near the R field (300m). At the end of the L field stay ahead on the winding path to the end of the wood (300m). Exit R across a neck of field to the track (30m).

④ Go L on the track (or the path R of it) to the houses at the top end of Crabtree Lane (400m).

Ⓢ *Short cut of 2km/1¼ miles: Turn R on the path past the houses (50m) then L round the garden and down beside the R field (200m). Turn R on the path in the wood below the field. Keep on along the hillside over a steep oblique cross path (500m) and ahead ➜⑨*

⑤ Turn L along the lane. Watch out for a path in the field R (200m) and cross the field obliquely L down to the middle of the bottom edge (100m). Go on through the trees and down the L edge of the next field to the road (450m).

⑥ Walk down the road L (100m). Opposite Chapel Farm turn R up the drive past the chapel ruins to the L bend at the wood (400m). ✦

⑦ Start up the path at the edge of the wood (30m) then turn R into the field. Follow the power cables down to the brow of the hill (250m) then bear L to follow the path at the bottom edge of the wood and up into another field (200m). Keep to the R edge to the next road (300m).

⑧ Walk down the road past the houses (150m). At the T-junction go L briefly (30m) then up the R field obliquely L to a slight dip, ¾ of the way along the top (350m) Carry on up through the wood to the cross path (80m). Turn L. ✛

⑨ Stay on this path over the downhill bridleway (150m) then winding and undulating to the next road (300m). Slighty L continue on the path up the other side (60m).

⑩ Watch out for the side path R to cut a corner to the wide path (80m). Turn R, curving L, to the bridleway (Connicut Lane) (120m). ❀ Cross it and carry on straight over the field to the gate of the Polesden Lacey garden (250m).

Ⓝ *National Trust members may go through the grounds: stay ahead to the drive (400m) then follow signs to the car park (300m).*

⑪ Non-NT walkers, turn R to the corner of the field (40m) and go through gates to the next field (30m). Aim obliquely L for the end of the trees (250m) and go round the corner to the main drive (250m). (The **Tea Room** is through the NT car park (150m) & L.

⑫ Walk along the drive or beside the R fence past the lodge to the R bend (450m). (Free car park L).

⑬ Cross to the edge of the field ahead and follow the path downhill L of the road (550m).

⑭ At the road junction cross the road ahead and continue up the track between fields (Admiral's Road) over the rise, past the 4-way junction (750m) to the next cross track (500m) where the track L leads to Downs Way (120m).

10 Norbury Park and Fetcham Downs

About 8 km/5 miles with an extension of 1½ km/1 mile; farmland and woods on chalk; one steep ascent. OS maps 1:25000 146 Dorking, 1:50000 187 Dorking.

Start at Bocketts Farm car park, TQ 155 549, near Leatherhead (groups need permission to park) or at Crabtree Lane car park, TQ 158 524, at Westhumble. Young Street car park on the A246, TQ 163 551, is close to the route.

Bocketts **Tea Rooms** 01372 363764   **The Running Horses** 01372 372279
The Stepping Stones 01306 889932

Linking walks
9★ 11★ 12✿

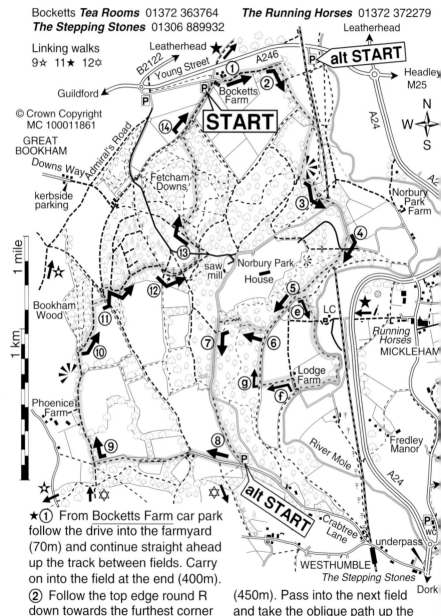

© Crown Copyright
MC 100011861

★① From Bocketts Farm car park follow the drive into the farmyard (70m) and continue straight ahead up the track between fields. Carry on into the field at the end (400m).

② Follow the top edge round R down towards the furthest corner (450m). Pass into the next field and take the oblique path up the slope L of a clump of trees to the top gateway (400m).

③ Don't enter the wood here but bear L down to the middle of the end of the field (100m); then go down through the wood (100m), over a cross path and up past the tunnel mouth L to the Norbury Hill drive (100m). Follow the drive down L to the field. Visible L across the Mole Gap is Cherkley Court. Watch out R for the oblique path rising over the grass (250m).

④ Bear R up this path to the old drive (80m). Cross to the path in the wood and go down past the tunnel mouth L (150m) to the side path L just before fields L (300m).

ⓔ *Extension of 1½ km/1 mile beside the River Mole: Turn back L on the side path in the wood (80m). Watch out through the trees for a stile into the field R and cross it (50m). In the field aim ½ L over the brow to the river bank at the farm bridge (100m). Cross the track to the next field and follow the river bank through the fields to the next bridge near Lodge Farm (800m).*

ⓕ *Outside the field follow the track R away from the bridge (100m). Just before the house turn back L and take the path between hedges up to the top of the fields (200m).*

ⓖ *Turn R on the path outside the fields (350m).* ➔⑥

⑤ Keep to the path ahead above the fields, past a path from the fields (100m) and on (200m).

⑥ Watch out for a small uphill path to a clearing in the trees. Go up via the top R corner of the clearing to a path along the hillside at the Druids' Grove yews (200m). Go R (60m) then L up the zigzag path to

the top of Norbury Hill (80m). See the view then walk away from the brow to the tarmac drive (100m).

⑦ Follow the drive L to the corner of a field R (500m). Where it bends down L stay ahead on the path beside the field down to Crabtree Lane car park (500m). ✿

⑧ Walk up the lane to the houses at the end (350m) and continue on the level path ahead to the next cross path (700m). ★

⑨ Turn R up over the brow of the hill. Carry on between fields, R of Phoenice Farm (400m) then under trees to Bookham Wood (300m).

⑩ Disregard paths ahead into the wood and turn R down round the edge of the field (350m).

⑪ Near the bottom of the field a track crosses R to a gate (80m). Pass through this gate, turn L and fork R. Very soon (40m) turn R up the side path in the trees and stay ahead, avoiding L turns, to the track with power lines (400m).

⑫ Turn R and look ahead. Over the track at the foot of the slope two paths rise across the grass L of the house. Take the one L of the electricity poles (300m). Near the top of the clearing bear L on the cross track from the edge of the trees over the vehicle track to a 5-way junction (100m).

⑬ Turn L on the bridleway (120m) and take the next side path R through the trees to Fetcham Downs. Stay ahead beside the trees over a cross path (100m) and down into the dry valley (600m).

⑭ In the trees at the very bottom turn R (100m) then continue on the parallel track beside the fields to Bocketts Farm (250m).

11 Leatherhead and Norbury Hill

About 7½ km/4½ miles with an extension of 2¾ km/1¾ miles to Mickleham. Farmland and woods, steep slopes. OS maps 1:25000 146 Dorking, 1:50000 187 Dorking.

Start from Young Street car park near the railway bridge on the A246, TQ 163 551. Bocketts Farm car park is on the route, TQ 156 549. In Mickleham there is roadside parking, TQ 170 533.

Linking walks 9❀ 10★ 13◈

Running Horse Leatherhead
☎ 01372 372081

Running Horses Mickleham
☎ 01372 372279

Bocketts ***Tea Room***
☎ 01372 363764

① At Young Street car park take the path away from the road and L to the River Mole (50m). Turn R. Follow the river bank to the end of the meadow (500m) and go on through the trees (100m). Continue on the track to the house (250m).

ⓔ *Extension of 2¾ km/1¾ miles to Mickleham: Bear L on the track (500m) and continue on the tarmac drive past Norbury Park Farm and over the river. Cross the A24 to 50m L of the Mickleham side road (Old London Rd) (500m).*

ⓕ *Enter the house drive at the end of the wall ◈ and stay ahead on the footpath between fences to Mickleham churchyard (250m).*

ⓖ *Turn R past the church to the road (100m). Take the lane beside the **Running Horses** and stay ahead to the A24 (400m), over the dual carriageway, along the lane opposite (100m) and over the railway lines to the farm (50m).*

22

When the main track bends L take the farm track down round L of the barns to the river (100m). Cross the bridge and continue up the track until it bends L (200m).

ⓗ *Turn R on the path up to the trees (100m) ★ and bear R on the path at the top of the fields (100m). Pass the side path R and go up through the wood to the old drive of Norbury Park near a bend (450m).*

ⓘ *Turn L. Don't go round the bend but stay ahead up the track eventually curving R beside the fence (300m). Cross the old drive and carry on along the fence to the tarmac drive (200m).* ➜③

② Turn R up the path R under the railway (450m). At the tarmac drive Ascend R to the fence (100m)

③ Continue on tarmac beside the fence of <u>Norbury</u> Park house (300m). When it bends L continue ahead past the track L from the sawmill (60m) and out of the wood to where horse tracks diverge L&R (150m). ❀ Take the R track to the crossing horse track (100m).

ⓐ *Another time, when you know the main paths: Just after the crossing horse track bear R on the diverging footpath through the trees and cross Fetcham Down to the 1st side path L (150m). Turn L then stay ahead through a narrow belt of trees (80m), over to the corner of the wood (100m) then beside it. Disregard side paths L (which re-join the horse track) until the path curves R at the very bottom (300m). Turn down the side path L in the trees and pass R of the little field to the brick stables (60m). Turn R.* ➜⑤

④ Stay ahead down to the vehicle track (400m) then down R to the 4-way junction at the fields (250m). Turn R on the bridleway between fields winding round behind the stables (100m). Stay ahead.

⑤ Use either the track next to the field or the shady parallel path 5m R of it up in the trees. Keep on to Bocketts Farm (800m).

⑥ At <u>Bocketts Farm</u> cross the main drive outside the gateway and go up the concrete track to the main road (100m). Cross to the track opposite. Go down between fields and curve L up to a T-junction near large buildings (600m).

⑦ Turn down R (150m) and take the first path L over the grass (150m). Cross the railway bridge and continue past the houses to the tarmac cross path (300m). Stay ahead on the tarmac drive curving past <u>Thorncroft</u> Manor to the river (300m). Don't cross this bridge.

⑧ Follow the path L along the river past sports fields to <u>Leatherhead Bridge</u> (550m). Walk out onto the bridge (50m). The **Running Horse** is up the street on the other side.

⑨ Return from the bridge and make for the Leisure Centre. Either go L, back along the river (250m) then cross the sports field R (250m) or continue along the pavement past the road junction (200m) and turn L on the side road before the railway bridge (300m). Take the tarmac path L of the Leisure Centre (200m) and cross the track.

⑩ Continue on the path eventually beside the river (400m) and under the road (200m). After the bridge (80m) turn R to the car park (50m).

12 Ranmore Common and Denbies Vineyard

About 8km/5 miles. North Downs, farmland and woods; hilly.
OS maps 1:25000 146 Dorking, 1:50000 187 Dorking.

Start from Crabtree Lane car park Westhumble, TQ 158 524, or from Denbies Hillside car park (NT/pay), TQ 142 153. Denbies Vineyard don't mind walkers using their car park (free), TQ 165 511.

The Stepping Stones 01306 889932
Denbies Restaurant 01306 876616

Linking walks
8✳ 9✦ 10✿ 14☆ 34✧

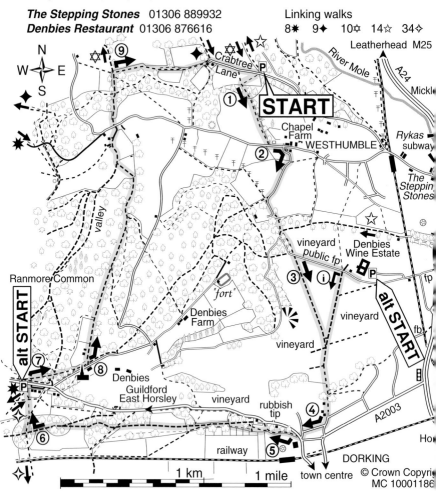

☆① Cross into the field below Crabtree Lane and make for the middle of the bottom edge (100m). Descend through the trees and go down the L edge of the next field to the road (450m).

② Walk down the road L (100m). At Chapel Farm turn R up the winding tarmac drive past the chapel ruins to the wood (500m). When the drive bends to the house up R stay ahead on the track in the trees (100m), over a cross track (NDW) into Denbies vineyard and down the R edge to the tarmac drive (200m).

24

ⓘ *If going to the vineyard visitor centre and restaurant turn L down the drive to the building (500m).*

③ Carry on across the vineyard to the gate at the tree-lined far edge (900m), along the track then the tarmac lane into <u>Dorking</u> (200m).

④ At the first street of houses bear R (70m). Turn R along Chalk Pit Terrace (150m) and L at the end down to Ranmore Road (40m).

⑤ Opposite, take the path into the trees (200m). After the house R when the path curves up R to the road, take the branch path L which rises to a straight major track just after another house (150m). Walk up the track L past a diverging downhill side track (400m), past an oblique cross path (600m) and through the wood (250m). Join the track from back R and go on though more wood (250m). ✧✷

⑥ After a break in the wood watch out for the cross path. Go straight up the steep path through the trees (100m). Avoid the diverging path R on the brow and go over Denbies

⤻ Opposite Denbies Hillside is the tower on Leith Hill, visible at a gap in the trees. Clearly in the same ridge are the peaks of Holmbury and Pitch Hills further R. Below is Westcott and the Redhill-Guildford-Reading railway. To the L (E) is Dorking with an obvious church spire. The town stands at the south end of the Mole Gap with Box Hill and the Downs continuing beyond.

<u>Hillside</u> to the NT car park which is on <u>Ranmore Common</u> (200m).

⑦ From the car park cross the road to the track at the trees (50m). Turn R (NDW) passing L of the house at the road junction (200m) and carry on past <u>Ranmore Church</u> converging on the road (300m).

⑧ Opposite the old school, turn L on the track in the trees, past a house. Stay ahead on this track until it enters fields (1300m). Keep on down past the farm buildings (300m). Follow the drive out to the road (150m). Go up the path in the field opposite into the trees. ✦ Ascend in the wood to the cross path from the fields L (350m). ✿

⑨ Take the path R along the top edge of the wood just below the field eventually joining Crabtree Lane at houses (650m). Continue on the lane to the car park (350m).

The Chalk beneath this walk is about 270m (890') thick. It was laid down as a deposit of coccoliths on the floor of an ocean over a period of 30m years ending 70m years ago. Coccoliths are 5 µm disks (1 µm=$^{1}/_{1000}$ mm) formed like elaborate tiles in the shells of a group of planktonic algae called the Coccolithophores. Most of these disks crumbled in the chalk but occasionally whole ones are found. Rarely the fossil of a whole alga is found. The electron microscope picture shows *W barnesæ* of the Upper Chalk. Coccoliths have distinctive shapes indicating hundreds of species. Geologists use them to correlate the ages of rocks around the world. Many species disappeared at the dinosaur/ammonite extinction.

 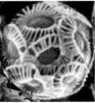

Watzaueri barnesæ   *Emeliana huxleyi*
Emeliana huxleyi, nicknamed Ehux, is the most widespread & studied living species. In algal blooms it forms white patches in ocean photographs as the coccoliths reflect sky light. They are crystalline calcium carbonate, calcite.

13 Mickleham Downs and Westhumble

About 7½ km/4¾ miles. An extension of 3½ km/2¼ miles and a short cut of 4 km/2½ miles can be used together. Steep slopes and fine views; a nasty road crossing. OS maps 1:25000 146 Dorking, 1:50000 187 Dorking.

Start from White Hill car park on Headley Lane, TQ 177 529, (NT/free) or from the roadside in Mickleham, TQ 170 533.

Linking walks 11◇ 14◆ 16✿ 17✪

The Running Horses ☎ 01372 372279
The William IV ☎ 01372 372590
Rykas Café ☎ 01306 884454

Cherkley Court

Leatherhead

Norbury Park

William IV

MICKLEHAM

Running Horses

Lodge Farm

River Mole

Crabtree Lane

Fredley Manor

Juniper Hall

tower

Rykas
WESTHUMBLE underpass
Polesden Lacey Bookham
The Stepping Stones Dorking

Headley Lane

Juniper Top
Juniper Bottom

Warren Farm

White Hill

START

On the brow fork L to the top of the ridge (100m). At the next path junction turn R across the the end of the ridge to the tower (100m).✦

② At the tower turn R down the path towards the distant Juniper Hall (150m). Turn L on the track at the bottom past a house and carry on down the drive to the road (450m).

③ Opposite, climb the steps beside the gates of Fredley Manor and continue on the path above the road past the end of Headley Lane R (250m) to the end (250m).

⑤ *Short cut of 4 km/2½ miles: carry on along the pavement to Mickleham Church (400m).* ✦ⓘ

ⓘ *If starting in Mickleham follow the L edge of the churchyard from opposite the **Running Horses** (100m). Go L on the first side path to the narrow road (150m) and on beside a field (100m). Turn R.* ✦⑩

① At White Hill car park walk away from the road up the Juniper Bottom track (300m). After the top of the field turn R on the first side path straight up the side (200m).

© Crown Copyright MC 100011861

26

④ Continue on pavement (50m). Take the side path L down to the trees and L down to the field below (100m). Follow the L edge (100m). In the next field continue to the *Mill Way* corner of the wall then cross 33 P to the gate (100m). ⑨ Headley Over the drive, slightly L, take the path between gardens to the A24 (200m).

⑤ Cross the dual carriageway slightly L and go down the track then under the railway (80m). Turn L and stay beside the railway over the River Mole (100m) and along the edge of the field to the road in Westhumble (450m).

⑥ Turn back R on Crabtree Lane past the chapel of ease. Watch out for access down to the field R (150m) then follow the L edge of the field to the corner (400m). Continue through the wood to the next field (300m). Fork R outside the field above the river (Norbury Park ahead). Eventually descend to a farm bridge (400m).

⑦ Turn L along the track from the bridge which twists L (100m) to pass the house. Keep on between fields (400m). When the track turns R stay ahead on the path to the wood (100m). Join the converging path and go on up through trees to the Norbury Hill old drive (500m). ✧

⑧ Turn R down the old drive and continue beside the new drive (250m). Bear R when the drive bends L and rejoin the level drive at the bottom (200m).

⑨ Turn R over the river. Cross the A24 to 50m L of the Mickleham side road (150m). At the end of the wall go along the drive past the house then the footpath (70m) and turn L.

⑩ Follow the side path behind gardens and stay ahead on the unmade road then on tarmac until it twists L to the A24 (250m).

⑪ Continue ahead up past one house (30m) then turn R up the stepped path between houses past the **William IV**. Carry on up over a level cross path (70m), steeply through the wood, round L past the end of the fenced conifer plantation to the oblique straight cross track (Downs Road/Stane Street)(500m).

ⓔ *Extension of 3½ km/2¼ miles: Turn L on the track along (R of) the fence. Keep to this track up round L & R bends, past a side path L at the end of the fence (550m) and on past a field R to a major cross path before fields (700m).*

ⓕ *Turn R. Stay on this path rising between the golf course and field, then through the wood to the car park at Mill Way (1000m).* ✿

ⓖ *Take the other bridleway away from the road. Stay on this track under trees past a side path L ✿ (850m) to the long narrow clearing of Mickleham Down (50m). Follow the L path along the middle (800m). 50m before the end trees take the side path L into the wood.* ➔⑬

⑫ Turn R (80m) then L up the next side path past the trig point to the long clearing on Mickleham Down (100m). Cross the grass on the small path R into the trees, 50m from the R corner (100m).

⑬ Follow the path through the wood to a 3-way junction (200m) and bear L (40m). At the next junction bear R along the brow of White Hill (200m) then descend the stepped path to the road opposite the car park (150m).

14 Box Hill and Denbies Vineyard

About 8½ km/5½ miles with extensions of 3 km/1¾ miles and 2 km/1¼ miles; steep slopes and splendid views.
OS maps 1:25000 146 Dorking, 1:50000 187 Dorking.

Start from the public car park near Burford Bridge, TQ 171 520, or Stepping Stones car park (NT/pay), TQ 170 513, or Denbies Vineyard (free), TQ 165 511.

Linking 8✿ 12☆ 13✦ 15☆ 34♣ 37✪ 38※

The Stepping Stones ☎ 01306 889932
Denbies Restaurant ☎ 01306 876616

① Take the uphill path at the end wall of the Burford Bridge Hotel. Don't stay on this path but go up the edge of the grass near the trees. Keep on ahead over the brow of Box Hill (300m) ☆ then less steeply (350m).
② When the track is close by L, join it via the diverging side path L through the trees. Continue up the track, past the fort, to the road (300m). Go R on the pavement or past

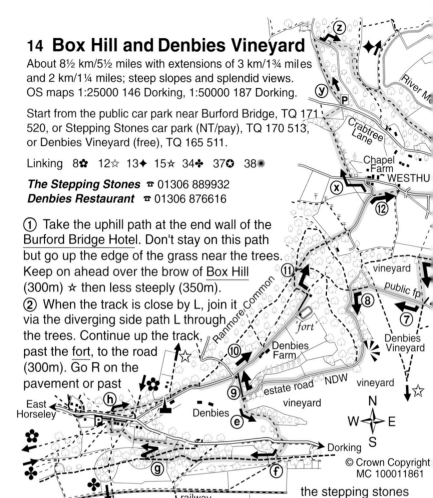

© Crown Copyright
MC 100011861

the National Trust café, wc & shop to the treeless edge of the hill and descend to the Salomons memorial view point and trig point (300m).✪※
③ Look down the slope to identify the paths that pass through the first hedge then follow the R one down to the second hedge (300m).
④ Turn R and continue through the trees, ultimately up round a bend to the stepped path (400m). Follow this path down L (200m). At the path junction on the flat area after the pillbox continue to the car park over the River Mole either via

the stepping stones ahead (300m) or via the footbridge R (100m) and L (300m).
⑤ From Stepping Stones car park cross the A24 to the L corner of the wood (80m). Follow the drive (NDW) beside the wood under the railway and past a house L (250m). Watch out for side paths in the trees. Pass a path R (100m) and go on to the cross path (350m).
⑥ Take the L path though Denbies Vineyard (300m). The large building L has a restaurant and display. ☆
⑦ Turn R up the drive to the bend (400m). Fork L up the steep track to a cross drive (150m).

⑧ Turn L. Follow the winding drive up the edge of the <u>North Downs</u> escarpment to the top of the wood (550m). Stay ahead to the track R after another tree clump (650m).

e Extension of 2¾ km/1¾ miles: Turn L down the path to the road (400m). Cross into the field and descend to the R corner (100m).

f Outside, go R on the track, past an oblique cross track (550m) to a converging side track R (350m). ♣

g Turn back R up the side track (300m) and take the 1st side path L round the bend and along the hill. Stay on the path over the grass of Denbies Hillside beside trees R (350m) and past, L of, the garden hedge (150m). ✿ Go round the hedge R to the road (50m).

h From the car park, cross the road to the edge of the trees (50m). Turn R on the horse track. Stay on it past <u>Ranmore</u> Church (400m) ☆ until it finally bends into the trees (200m) then follow the road to the L bend (250m). Stay ahead. ➔⑩

⑨ Go up the R track to the drive at the lodge (150m) and turn R.

⑩ Follow the drive past Denbies Farm (200m) and the next house (<u>fort</u> not visible) (400m). Keep on to the house at the wood (100m).

⑪ Follow the L bend in the trees then a R bend (100m). Bear R on the converging track (100m). Avoid L & R branch paths and pass over the brow of the hill, down across a track (300m) then beside a field L to tarmac (150m). Turn L down the winding drive. Watch out for a side path down R on the L bend (400m).

x Extension of 2 km/1¼ miles: Stay on the drive down to <u>Chapel Farm</u> (100m) and turn L up the road to the 1st field R (100m). Go up the R edge (350m) and on through the trees (100m). In the next field aim for the top R corner (150m) and cross the road.

y From Crabrtree Lane car park follow the path in the wood beside the field to the tarmac drive (450m).

z Turn back R down the drive watching out for a path L (100m). Drop to the next path (20m) and descend R (350m). ✦ At the field stay with the hedge round down to the corner (150m) then bear R through the wood to the next field (300m). Follow the R edge almost to the end (500m) then cut across to pass L of the house, beside the railway, to the road (100m). ✦⑬

⑫ Go down the side path (200m). Turn R on the road, down, up, down through <u>Westhumble</u> (500m).

⑬ Cross the railway bridge and go down the road past the **Stepping Stones** (450m) to the A24 (50m).

⑭ Cross via the underpass L (70m) then follow the pavement L over Burford Bridge and round past the hotel (250m).

15 Box Hill, Juniper Top and the River Mole

About 8 km/5 miles with an extension of 1½ km/¾ mile; hilly North Downs walk with fine views. OS maps 1:25000 146 Dorking, 1:50000 187 Dorking.

Start from Stepping Stones car park (NT/pay), TQ 170 513, or the free public car park near Burford Bridge, TQ 171 520, or the free Zig Zag car park. White Hill car park (free) and the NT (pay) car parks on Box Hill are near the route.

The Smith & Western
☎ 01737 841666
The Watermill
☎ 01306 883248
Rykas Café
☎ 01306 884454

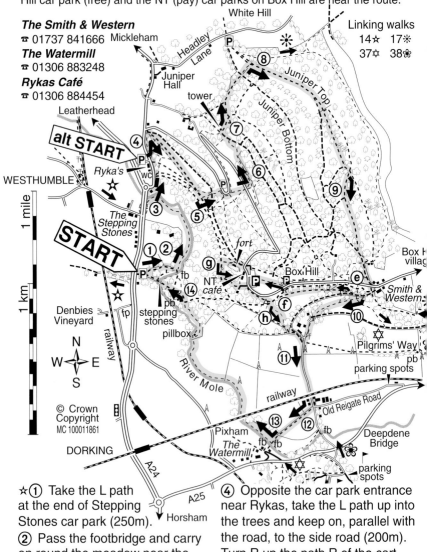

① Take the L path at the end of Stepping Stones car park (250m).

② Pass the footbridge and carry on round the meadow near the River Mole to the A24 (700m).

③ Go along the pavement R, over Burford Bridge then round the side road past the hotel (300m).

④ Opposite the car park entrance near Rykas, take the L path up into the trees and keep on, parallel with the road, to the side road (200m). Turn R up the path R of the cart track, past Flint Cottage L. Go up the slope (Box Hill) to where the gradient becomes less steep and other paths converge R (500m).

30

⑤ After this convergence watch out for paths L to the edge of the hill. Follow one of these down over the track to pass R of the hairpin bend in the road below (200m).

⑥ From the hairpin bend take the path straight up the E side of the valley (120m). Cross the road up to the trees above (40m). Follow the edge of the trees L ultimately to the parallel track out of the trees. Keep on (L) to Broadwood tower (450m) where Juniper Hall is visible below.

⑦ Turn R across the end of the hill (120m) and go down the next side path L (100m). Join the converging path into Juniper Bottom (200m). (White Hill car park down L 300m). Go up the path opposite and across to the ascending path (100m). ✲

⑧ Go up the slope R, Juniper Top. Near the wood, aim for the L way into the trees (600m). Stay on this path past a side track R (400m) to an oblique cross path (50m).

⑨ Bear R on the cross path. Stay on this path, past a side track R (200m), up to the converging major track (from Juniper Bottom)(350m). Carry on to the road (250m). Cross into the trees R of the **Smith & Western** (40m) and start down the sunken track R. ✿✿

ⓔ *Extension of 1½ km/¾ miles round the Box Hill features: Watch out for the 2nd access L into the field (120m). Just after it (30m) take the diverging path R up the bank. Stay ahead above the sunken path, through the trees to the next field, and along the top (450m).*

ⓕ *Just before the corner at the trees ascend R through a gate and cross the road (50m). Bear L over the clearing (Donkey Green) and*

cross the road to the National Trust shop, wc and food kiosk (300m). Take the side track from the road, R of the buildings. At the end of the fort (50m) turn L and L again (70m).

ⓖ *In the trees on the edge of the hill turn L on the path, past the Labilliere memorial (50m) and L at the next side track (70m) past the Logie Baird plaque to the road (200m). Walk down the pavement R and drop to the Saloman memorial and trig point (150m).*

ⓗ *Identify the hedge below and make for the bottom L end (200m). Follow downhill paths (200m).* ➧⑪

⑩ Watch out for the first access L to the field (70m) and descend the path diverging from the sunken track (Ranmore Church up ahead across Mole Gap) (350m). Turn R on the track near houses (15m) & L down the edge of the field (150m). Continue down the drive (30m).

⑪ Keep on down the road under the railway to the bend (500m).

⑫ Climb the bank R into the field and follow the path down to the river opposite Castle Mill (400m). (**Watermill** Inn over bridge 150m)

⑬ Turn R before the footbridge and follow the river bank under the railway (300m) and on to the end of the fields (700m). Outside the last field, before the pillbox, take the path winding up through the trees to the stepped path (300m).

⑭ Go down the stepped path L to the level area (100m) (side paths R lead to the river footbridge). Keep on over the stepping stones (100m). ★ Either stay ahead to Stepping Stones car park (100m) or, if continuing, turn R and keep to the river bank (180m). ➧②

16 Headley, Heath and Mickleham Downs

About 8½ km/5¼ miles. A short cut of 1¾ km/1 mile and extension of 800m/½ mile can be used together. A hilly North Downs walk.
OS maps 1:25000 146 Dorking, 1:50000 187 Dorking.

Start at Headley Heath Main car park (NT/pay), TQ 205 538. Free parking places on the route are Cockshot car park, TQ 188 535, Mill Way car park, TQ 193 545, and at The Cock in Headley, TQ 204 548.

Linking 13✿ 17✳ 18✺

The Cock ☎ 01372 377258

Mill Way

alt START

Lodgebottom Road

alt START

White Hill

Cockshot Cottage

Warren Farm

High Ashurst

Headley Road

Headley Heath

Bellasis

The Cock

HEADLEY

N
W   E
S

© Crown Copyright MC 100011861

1 km   1 mile

parking spots

The Box Tree

BOX HILL village

✳ⓔ *Extension of 800m/½ mile:*
At the end furthest from the cricket field, leave the main car park by the gate nearest the road. Follow the track almost parallel with the road (150m). After the fence stay ahead on the R track past Brimmer Pond R (500m) (oblique paths L lead to Brimmer car park 200m). Carry on (200m) to the major ½R side track, (35m before a major cross track). ✳
ⓕ *Bear R on this side track. Stay ahead over a cross track (from the parallel major track) (120m), into the valley (150m), up over another cross track (50m) and round R to a 6-way junction (200m).* ✳

ⓖ *Turn R on the main long straight path which soon emerges from the trees and descends the end of the ridge with steps near the bottom (850m). Turn L.* ➔③
① At Headley Heath main car park take the path directly away from the road at the L corner. Stay ahead between ponds (sometimes dry in summer) (350m) and past a side track converging L (200m) to the complex of tracks & paths (200m).

32

② Turn down the lesser R track (50m) then L on the cross track. Stay on this path to the wood at the end of the ridge (230m) then descend L into the valley with steps at the bottom (170m). Turn R.

③ Follow the valley track round the L curve past a field R (100m) then go up the steep side path R beside the boundary fence and round a L bend (130m). ✿ Turn R on the side path below the wall (of High Ashurst) and descend under trees then between fields. Cross the road to Cockshot car park (450m).

④ From the car park take the path outside the adjacent field round to a side path at the corner (200m).

Ⓢ *Short cut of 2 km/1¼ miles: From the field corner take the steep side path R to the top of the ridge at the E end of Mickleham Downs grassland (350m). Turn R.* ➳⑧

⑤ Carry on round the corner and rise steeply briefly (100m). Keep on along the flank of White Hill to the the first clear path junction (900m).

⑥ Turn R on the side path and R again (40m). Keep on to the grass of Mickleham Downs (300m).

⑦ Go R along the middle of the grass corridor to the end (850m).

⑧ Keep on along the almost level path through the wood to the road, Mill Way (950m).

⑨ From Mill Way car park take the track beside the road (200m) then cross and follow the track away from the road watching out for the side path R into the field (100m).

⑩ In the field follow the L edge briefly (30m) then turn L along the top edge of the side field (100m). Stay ahead from field to field and down to the road (350m).

⑪ At the lane junction go R down the descending lane, watching out for a side path L just after the farm drive R and cottage L (200m).

⑫ Go up the path between fields and gardens (300m). When the path ahead leads to a field below houses, turn up around the field to the road in Headley (150m). Cross and follow the drive L of **The Cock** (50m). Inside the churchyard turn R & L to the back gate (80m).

⑬ Outside, turn R. Stay ahead over the fields crossing a track (200m), a drive (220m) and more fields (220m). ❋

⑭ Don't cross into the field before the house with barns L but turn R along the edge (150m). After the next house bear L to the drive (20m) and R along it (150m).

⑮ Go L on the track above the road (40m) then diverge from the road under the trees (150m). Cross the next drive, slightly R, and take the other drive ahead L of the cricket field (170m). After the pavilion turn R and cross the road to Headley Heath car park (70m).

Headley, like its Hampshire and Berkshire namesakes, probably derives its name from the Anglo-Saxon for *heath* and *clearing*, a break in the forest that had become heath or a clearing in heath that had become the settlement. In the Domesday Book it is HALLEGA in the Hundred of Copthorne. The present church, St Mary, was built in the 1850s in 13th century style. The grotto in the churchyard constructed from stone of the previous church has 15th century carving but the records go back to the 13th century. Headley Court, north of the village, is a military rehabilitation centre but was a WWII HQ of Canadian Forces in Europe.

17 Headley Heath and Box Hill

About 9 km/5½ miles with an extension of 1½ km/1 mile.
Very steep slopes; long views; woods and chalk grassland.
OS maps 1:25000 146 Dorking, 1:50000 187 Dorking.

Start from White Hill car park, TQ 177 529.
Headley Heath Brimmer car park (NT/pay)
is on the the extension, TQ 206 532.

13❂ 15✳ 16✾ 18✦ 37✳ 38★

Smith & Western 01737 841666
The Box Tree 01737 845996

❂✳① At White Hill car park go up
the track from the road (70m) then
bear L through the gate up the path
to Juniper Top. Watch out for a side
path L into the trees (100m). Follow
it to a clearing and on through the wood
(450m). After the fork descend L to the
edge of the field and stay ahead, across
the end of the valley field (300m), along the
track above the farm until it curves R (250m)
then along the fence to the next valley (100m).
② Cross the valley drive and go up the winding
drive opposite. Continue through High Ashurst
round to the walled exit gateway (700m).
③ Turn L outside the wall. Go past a path L
(30m), steeply down and round R to the valley
bottom in Headley Heath (100m). Turn L on
the valley track curving R near a field (100m).
ⓔ *Extension of 1½ km/1 mile:*
Keep to this path which rises out
of the valley to become a ridge path
(450m). At the complex track
junction on top stay ahead to the
next major side track R (200m). ✦
ⓕ *Turn R on the side track and*
continue to its end (650m).
ⓖ *Turn L on the wide track to*
Brimmer Pond L (100m) and take
the side path ½R through the
trees to the car park (200m).
ⓗ *From the S exit of Brimmer car*
park, take the track into the trees
near the road (250m). When it
bends R stay ahead on the smaller
winding path out through the fence
(70m). Go on through the trees,
along the reservoir fence L (300m)
and the R edge of the field (200m).
ⓘ *Turn R up the road (80m) and*
take the footpath L between the
fields (300m). Carry on over the
brow of the hill down through the
yew wood then down beside a
garden (300m). On the drive turn R
(60m) then L downhill as far as the
next cluster of houses (100m).

34

path. Stay ahead through a 6-way junction (500m), over a major track (200m), through the fence (20m) along the L edge in wood (350m).

⑤ At the end turn R into Surrey Hills (chalet) Park (20m) and make for the shops in Box Hill village as follows: ahead (40m), R (100m), L to staggered cross-roads (170m), ahead (65m) then on a footpath to the road (50m). Turn L to the pub (200m).

⑥ Opposite the **Box Tree** follow the track into the trees (200m) and round the bend. Stay ahead, R of the reservoir avoiding paths L. The path curves down L and becomes very steep through yew hanger to a major cross path (600m).★✳ Turn R

⑦ Keep on, rising (400m).

⑧ Just before the field L (near houses R) take the side path L (NDW) over the bank (see memorial R) carry on down below fences to a converging path (350m). Continue down yew hanger watching out for a stepped path up R (300m).

⑨ Go up the stepped path round to a track junction (70m) and fork R. Keep on to the end at a fence (400m) then descend L (30m) and turn R. Carry on along the wooded hillside (350m). Cross the sunken track below the **Smith & Western** to the road R (30m). ✳

⑩ Follow the path opposite to the vehicle cross track (450m).

⑪ Turn R and keep to the track to the end of the wood (850m). Stay ahead down the ridge path, Juniper Top, to White Hill car park (800m).

ⓙ *Turn back R on the rough road (NDW) past more houses and go on up through trees (300m). At the drive from the limekiln towers L join the path L of the hedge (80m) then rejoin the undulating NDW. ★*
Keep on below old chalk workings (400m), round a L bend into trees (100m), round a R bend, to a steep cross path (200m) and ahead. ◆⑦

④ *Turn R on the steps up the ridge path (400m). At the fork take the L*

35

18 Headley Heath towards Buckland

About 8½ km/5¼ miles; an extension of 4 km/2½ miles. Farmland and woods; steep slopes; fine views. OS maps 1:25000 146 Dorking, 1:50000 187 Dorking.

Start from Headley Heath main car park (NT/pay), TQ 205 538. In Buckland, on the extension, there are parking spots at the green and shops, TQ 221 508.

Linking walks   16✳   17✦   19✿   38★

The Red Lion ☎ 01734 843336

① From Headley Heath main car park go round the cricket field and on to the end of the drive (250m). Cross slightly R and continue on the path under trees to the road (150m).

② Stay on the track above the road (40m) round to the 2nd house (40m) then follow the path in the field along the R edge (150m). After the path crossing the field, continue ahead R of the fence to the track at Heath Farm (150m).

③ Go R (80m) then take the side path L skirting the farmyard to the large field (60m). Go along the R edge (400m), L round the corner into the valley (400m), up the track in

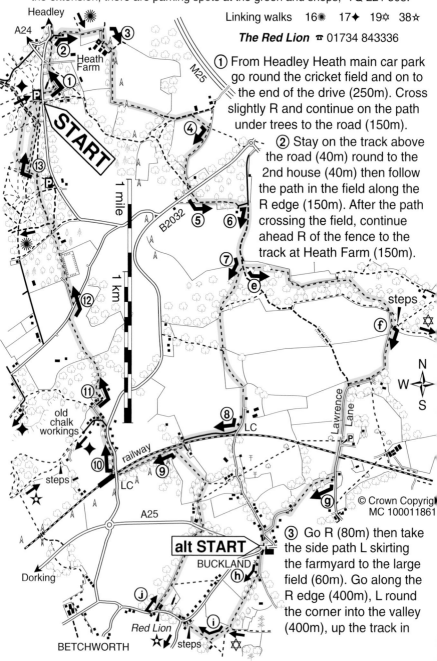

© Crown Copyright
MC 100011861

the trees (100m) and L of the field. Watch out for a side path R (120m).

④ *Take the path ½R across the field (150m) and turn R along the edge to the trees (300m). Go on to the path junction (200m) and L to the road (30m). Cross.*

⑤ Keep on opposite (80m). Bear L beside the field and join a house drive to the broad track (400m).

⑥ Go R on this level byway to the North Downs escarpment (400m) and down to a path junction (50m).

ⓔ *Extension of 4 km/2½ miles: Turn L on the bridleway which winds and undulates past an uphill side path L (750m) to join the NDW above the next fields (400m). ✿*

ⓕ *Round the bend (20m) fork R down to the fields. Descend to the clump of trees (300m) then bear R along the edge of the field to the lane (300m). Walk down the lane, over the railway (450m) to the foot-path R at the next house R (150m).*

ⓖ *Follow the path parallel with the R hedge into the next field (200m) and ahead L of a garden (250m), then the lane to Buckland village green (300m). Cross the A25.*

ⓗ *At Buckland church walk away from the A25 (50m) and L along Dungates Lane (150m). At the gate bear R on the footpath through the trees and between fields (400m).*

ⓘ *When the path bends L, enter the field R and cross obliquely to the trees R of the house ahead (150m). Turn R on the path outside the fields and drop to the road (200m). ☆ Walk down the road L to the **Red Lion** (250m).*

ⓙ *Go up the pub drive, on beside the trees over the rise (200m) and down to the A25 (400m). Cross to*

the path opposite and follow L edges to the end of the 2nd field (300m). Go L through the gateway, obliquely past a hedge end L (30m) and house R to the far L corner at the trees and railway (300m). ✦⑨

⑦ Diverge R on the side path, up briefly, then down to fields (350m). Go straight down the first, obliquely L in the next (500m). Stay ahead on the track then lane (300m).

⑧ Just before the railway take the track R (400m). Turn L under the bridge then immediately R# beside the railway in the field (100m).

⑨ Outside the fields follow the railway above the cutting and down to Betchworth Station (450m).

⑩ Cross the road then the railway and take the path above the road up to the track L with houses, The Coombe (350m). ✦ Turn L. Stay ahead up the tarmac drive (150m) but not up the path at the R bend.

⑪ Go round the bend past two houses (50m) then L up the steep path between gardens and trees (300m). On top keep on between fields to the road (300m).

⑫ Go R down the road to the drive L (80m) and take the path R of it in the field (200m). Carry on under trees L of the reservoir to the corner of Headley Heath (300m). Follow the path away from the fence (70m) then turn L (40m) ✳ and take the 1st R. Follow this bridleway until past Brimmer car park R (300m).

⑬ Turn L on the cross track from the car park, over another broad track (50m) and out of the trees Turn R on the 1st (30m) or 2nd (70m) cross path. Keep on outside the edge of the trees and over tracks to the main car park (500m).

19 **Reigate Heath, Buckland and Colley Hill**

About 9 km/5¾ miles with a little extension of 450m/¼ mile; a North Downs walk; farmland and the steep escarpment; short but very steep paths; grand views. OS maps 1:25000 146 Dorking, 1:50000 187 Dorking.

Start from the Reigate Heath car park, Flanchford Road, TQ 239 502.

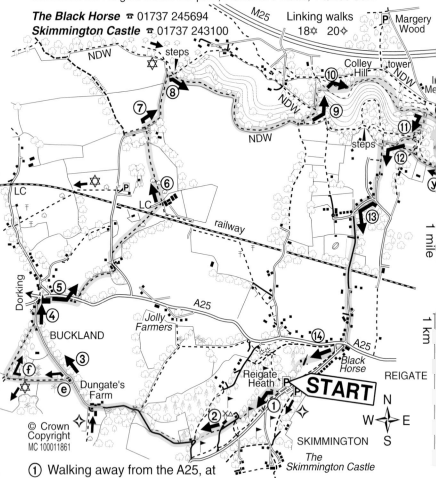

The Black Horse ☎ 01737 245694
Skimmington Castle ☎ 01737 243100

Linking walks 18✿ 20◇

① Walking away from the A25, at the end of the R car park take the path away from Flanchford Road though the trees (50m) then follow the edge of the trees L (200m). After the bridge L cross to the rising path in the scrub and go up to the house (100m). Walk along the track L of the house past the windmill and clubhouse to the junction with the converging club drive (150m).

② R of the drive, aim down (GW) across heath and fairway to the nearest house in the trees (200m). Cross the boundary track of Reigate Heath and take the track L of the house between fields to the stream, ahead over a bridge (500m), up to Dungates Farm (300m) and along the tarmac lane to the next house (300m).

38

(e) *Little extension of 450m/¼ mile: Take the path L (GW) after the house, straight across the fields to the next cross path (450m).* ✿

(f) *Turn R to the lane (400m).*

③ Continue on the lane (400m).

④ Stay ahead into Buckland (150m). Turn R to the A25 (50m).

⑤ Go through the churchyard L of the church and out to the A25 (80m). Follow the pavement R (200m). Just after the drive of Buckland Court, cross to the fields and follow the footpath away from the road R of the hedge (300m). At the corner go out towards the house and along the drive L to the road (80m). Walk up the road L (70m) then enter the R field. Cross obliquely L to the hedge bend opposite (100m) and continue L of the hedge (150m). When it bends away slightly R, bear L a bit along the middle, between the garden L and the hedge R, to the railway crossing (250m). On the other side, cross the field to the corner near the barns (100m).

⑥ Cross the farm drive to the next field and make for the top R corner in the trees at an angle midway between the garden trees L and the distant houses R (400m). Go through the belt of trees and over the drive into the next field (100m).

⑦ Follow the edge R to the end of the trees (120m) then turn L up the edge into the trees on the North Downs escarpment (300m).

⑧ Turn R up the side path (30m) and R along the contour path, the Norh Downs Way, just above the fields. Pass round a R bend (500m) and carry on to the next path junction (600m).

⑨ Bear L up the steep path (NDW) (150m). At the L bend take the side path ahead R of the fence up steps (120m) then R, almost level, to the grassland on Colley Hill (50m).

⑩ Walk out from the trees, slightly uphill, until you cross a path. Look along the hilltop R. Follow any of the paths curving along the middle of the grass but when you see the line of trees aim for the bottom end at the brow (600m). Keep on along the brow to the steep path R at the end of the scrub below (200m).

(x) *If this descent is too slippery: Continue on the brow to the end of the grass (200m) then follow the wide path down R (150m). After the Simpson Memorial (30m), diverge R down the side path (150m).*

(y) *Turn R down the broad path under trees beside fields (300m). On the R curve fork L down into the field ahead (30m).* ➔⑫

⑪ Go straight down the steep path (100m). Just before the trees, bear R round the edge of the trees to the major path across the foot of the grassland (100m). Slighly L take the path through the trees into the field below (20m).

⑫ Go down the field to the bottom end then L down the path outside then the drive to the road (400m).

⑬ Turn R and fork L down beside the wood (200m) then take the track down L. Stay ahead across the railway (350m) to tarmac, over a rise and down to the A25 opposite the **Black Horse** (500m).

⑭ Cross the grass into the trees behind the cricket pavilion (300m) and make your way through the network of paths, converging on the road L to the car park (250m).

20 Skimmington, Reigate Priory and Wonham

About 8½ km/5¼ miles with an extension of 1¼ km/¾ mile; undulating farmland and heath; fairly shady. OS maps 1:25000 146 Dorking, 1:50000 187 Dorking.

Start from the Reigate Heath car park, Flanchford Road, TQ 239 502, or join the route from Reigate through Priory Park.   Linking walks 19✧ 40✴ 42✴

The Black Horse ☎ 01737 245694   **Skimmington Castle** ☎ 01737 243100
The Jolly Farmers ☎ 01737 221355   **Pavilion Cafe** ☎ 01737 240050

© Crown Copyright MC 100011861

① At the Flanchford Road car parks walk away from the A25 on the diverging path in the trees L of the road. Keep on to the lane at houses (400m). Fork R up towards the **Skimmington Castle** but soon (40m) diverge L on the sandy path over the knoll L of the pub (100m) and down (250m). At the tarmac lane go L between trees and up almost to the barns (300m).

② Just after the house R turn L on the track between fields at the foot of the slope. Keep on round a R curve (500m) to the next road at the edge of Reigate (200m). Cross

into the trees and go on to the lake in Priory Park (70m).

ⓔ *Extension of 1¼ km/¾ mile: Follow the hard path L past the pond (200m) then cross the grass R to the foot of the hill (200m). Turn L along the edge of the trees or on the shady path 20m above (300m).*

ⓕ *At the beacon (basket on pole) turn R up the path in the wood almost to the next road (350m).*

ⓖ *At the highest point turn back R up the steepest side path to the Randal Vogan Memorial and trig point (150m). Carry on along the main ridge path (350m). ↦④*

③ Turn R round the lake (50m) then find the path away from the lake, over cross paths, straight up the hillside to the ridge path (300m). Turn R.

40

④ Follow the ridge to the end and drop to the road (400m). Go down Littleton Lane opposite past fields and through the wood (500m). Round the L bend continue on the Littleton Manor Farm drive (150m).

⑤ After the barn R diverge on the side track R which skirts the farm buildings. Stay on the track until it bends up R (350m) then enter the field ahead and make for the bottom L corner (150m). Carry on between the field L and the garden of Littleton Manor R (200m). Cross the road and follow the track down to the next farm (200m) and on past one more field (100m).

⑥ Turn L into the next field. Follow the L edge round the corner (100m) and on past trees to a pillbox L (300m). Cross the hedge but continue beside it. When it bends R (100m), stay ahead across a L bulge of the field (in a loop of the River Mole) and along the L edge to the corner (150m). ✳

⑦ Outside the field go L past the pillbox to see the river at the Rice Bridge (50m) then return and keep on along the winding path between fields (200m). Turn into the L field just before the garden hedge L, and follow the R edge to the end near a river bend (350m). Continue in the same direction along the next field towards a distant building in trees Wonham Mill (200m). Pass R of the pill box then aim 50m L of the mill to a gate at the trees (150m). Go out to the road (50m) and L round the R bend (50m).

⑧ Turn R into the trees behind the mill (30m) then take the side path L past (L of) the mill pond to the large field (50m). Keep on through the middle of paddocks to a hedge bend (250m) and on along the hedge to the road at Dungate's Farm (150m). ✧

⑨ Turn R on the tarmac and continue on the winding track down over the bridge (350m).

⑩ At the bend in the stream take the side path L into the field. Follow the edge to a path junction (500m).

⑪ Bear R across a corner of the field and carry on at the L edge (200m) then between fields (300m).

⑫ Just before the road take the path R, over a drive, into Reigate Heath to the cart track (80m). Go straight up the path opposite past the barrow (60m) then turn L past the higher barrow to the complex track junction (60m). Take the broad path away from the A25 curving L down through the edge of the trees, soon above the golf course R, to the car park (250m).

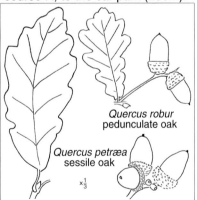

Quercus robur
pedunculate oak

Quercus petræa
sessile oak

×⅓

The British oak is not one species but two. They live side by side but usually one species predominates. In Surrey most are pedunculate oak, *Quercus robur*, with acorns on stalks. Sessile oak, *Quercus petræa*, has stalkless acorns in a cluster at the tip of a twig. The leaf stalks are vice versa, about 1 cm in *Q.petræa* while *Q.robur* has almost stalkless leaves.

21 Friday Street and Holmbury Hill

About 9¼km/5¾ miles with an extension of 800m/½ mile to Abinger Church; a hilly Greensand walk mainly through woods and hilltop heath.
OS maps 1:25000 146 Dorking 1:50000 187 Dorking.

Start from Friday Street car park, TQ 125 457, or from the kerbside in Holmbury St Mary near the *Royal Oak*, TQ 109 445.

The Stephan Langton ☎ 01306 730775   **The Kings Head** ☎ 01306 730282
The Royal Oak ☎ 01306 730120   **The Abinger Hatch** ☎ 01306 730737

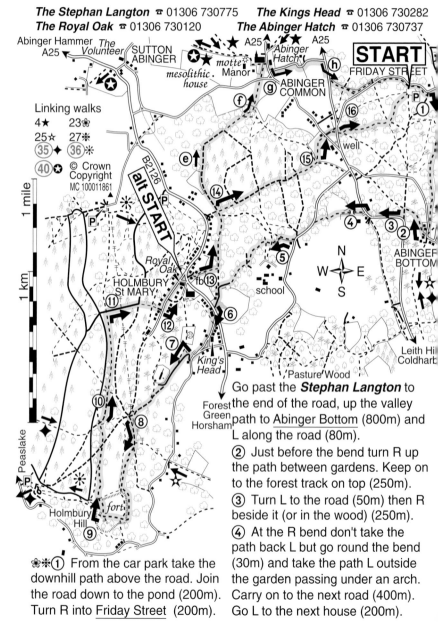

Go past the **Stephan Langton** to the end of the road, up the valley path to Abinger Bottom (800m) and L along the road (80m).

② Just before the bend turn R up the path between gardens. Keep on to the forest track on top (250m).

③ Turn L to the road (50m) then R beside it (or in the wood) (250m).

④ At the R bend don't take the path back L but go round the bend (30m) and take the path L outside the garden passing under an arch. Carry on to the next road (400m). Go L to the next house (200m).

⌘✳①① From the car park take the downhill path above the road. Join the road down to the pond (200m). Turn R into Friday Street (200m).

⑤ Take the path R beside the garden (100m). After the garden, fork L. Stay ahead on the winding and undulating path through the wood (300m). At the foot of the slope, on a cross track, turn L & R to carry on in the same direction through trees, then on the track bending L past the lodge to the road in Holmbury St Mary (400m). Cross to the pavement. ☆

⑥ Turn L (30m), then R up the side road (200m). At the **Kings Head**, fork R and keep on up to the house R on the L bend (200m).

⑦ Before the house turn back R up the steep cricket field track and round L (50m). Keep on ahead, passing L of the cricket field (300m) to the 5-way track junction (300m).

⑧ Turn L along the almost level track to a slight bend with L & R side paths 30m apart (200m). Go up the R side path then stay on the edge of Holmbury Hill, into a dip and on beside the fort (500m). Pass R round the corner of the hill and along the brow then turn down L to the Bray memorial seat and view point (150m). ✳◆

⑨ Go back up the slope past the seat and follow the track away from the edge. Stay ahead over the fort ramparts (150m) and a wide oblique cross track (350m) to the next cross paths (120m).

⑩ Turn R on the path curving L to the former direction down the slope to the major cross track (750m).

⑪ Turn R along the track (250m). At the T-junction on the edge of the hill drop down the steep path to the road in Holmbury St M (150m).

⑫ Walk down the road L to the **Royal Oak** (250m).

⑬ Cross the main road from the middle of the triangular green and go along the drive L of the garden wall (50m) then turn R behind the garden. Carry on round L (20m), over a stream and through the wood to a large footpath (200m). Follow it L to the track (400m).

ⓔ *Extension of ¾ km/½ mile to Abinger Church: take the track ahead round the edge then into the wood (600m). At the R bend, take the path ahead to the fork (150m).*

ⓕ *Bear L then ascend to the field (100m) and go straight up to the road (200m). Cross and go on to* Abinger Church *(100m) opposite the* **Abinger Hatch**. ★

ⓖ *Turn R back along the road past the pond (80m) and go down the next side road L into a dip and up to the main road (400m).*

ⓗ *Go up the road R (120m) and take the path L (120m). Fork L down towards the road (100m) and go on L of the road (100m). Join the road briefly (30m). Watch out for the path up the bank R of the road and follow it over the rise to the Friday Street car park (250m).*

⑭ Disregard the path R just before the track but turn R up the steep path from the track junction (150m). Stay ahead through the undulating fire break over the top and down into the trees to the field (650m)

⑮ Follow the path L at the field fence round R to the road (200m).

⑯ Cross the green (50m) and bear R to the path over the next road. Just into the wood (40m), fork L soon descending steeply to a 5-way path junction (350m). Ascend the ½L path to the Friday Street car park (250m).

22 Wotton and the North Downs

About 8km/5 miles; a short cut of 2½km/1½ miles and an extension of 2km/1¼ mile; farmland and woods; short steep slopes; splendid views; good in winter. OS maps 1:25000 146 Dorking, 1:50000 187 Dorking.

Start at the car park behind the *Wotton Hatch*, TQ 125 476. Abinger Roughs car park, TQ 111 480, and White Downs car park, TQ 114 494, are near the route.

Linking walks 2✳ 3★ 4✳ 8✿ 23✳ 34✵

The Wotton Hatch
☎ 01306 887694

From the **Wotton Hatch**, cross the main road and follow the drive towards <u>Wotton</u> Church (300m).
① Take the path skirting L of the churchyard, between fields and down into the wood (250m), then over another field to the track junction in the valley (300m).

② Slightly L, take the farm track up past the barns. Keep to the winding edge of the forest (700m). Eventually the track bends R (70m) then L (200m) to the road. ✳
③ Go R on the road over the railway bridge (100m) and up round the steep L & R bends to the <u>pillbox</u> L at the roadside (450m).

44

④ Just before the pillbox take the steep path L up round a R bend to the cross path (<u>North Downs Way</u>) (100m) ✭ Turn R, past a pillbox, up the NDW (200m). On top, when the NDW bends down R, take the side path ahead curving up L between disused chalk pits to join the next track on a bend (150m). Follow the track R past the reservoir (150m).✳

⑤ Turn R on the main forest track past a side track L (50m) and a little path L (from White Downs car park) (250m) to the road (70m). Slightly L (20m) climb the winding forest track on the other side up to the L bend on top (100m).

⑥ Just after the side path L and just before the bend, take the side path R (80m) then fork R. Keep on through the beech wood and drop down the bank to the corner of the field and the NDW (200m).

⑦ Go L along the NDW at the top of the field to the downhill cross track in a cleft at a pillbox (400m).

Ⓢ *Short cut of 2½km/1½ miles: Turn R down the track or the path beside it (100m). Watch out for a side path L straight down the slope in line with hedges below and drop down it to the track (200m). Stay ahead along the L edge of the field (150m), over the railway, down through the valley (still at L edge) and up beside the wood to a broad track (500m) and over the ridge down to Vale houses (200m).* ➔⑫

⑧ Follow the NDW L up the track (150m) and R on next side path R. Keep to the brow of the hill to the next descending track (700m). ✿

ⓔ *Extension of 2km/1¼ miles: Stay on the NDW through the wood to the 1st field R (700m).* ✪

Ⓕ *Enter the field and follow the L edge soon descending beside the wood to the 2nd cross path (450m).*

Ⓖ *Descend steeply round the little wood (100m), over the level track and down to the railway (150m).*

Ⓗ *Don't cross. Go R along the field (200m), through the NT farm yard (50m) and up the track to the junction (300m). Stay ahead to the sloping cross path (250m).* ➔⑩

⑨ Descend R, round a L bend to the level track along the bottom of the escarpment (350m) and turn L to the sloping cross path (70m).

⑩ Go down the path between hedges and over the railway lines (150m). Keep on along the track (150m). On the bend just before the hedge corner L, turn R on the path into the trees and L over the brook to the next field (30m). Stay ahead beside the hedge (50m). When it bends L, go straight up the field towards the L end of the wood above (200m), ahead through the trees (100m) and down the L edge of the next field. Cross the brook to the road (250m).

⑪ Follow the road R up to the next houses R (200m) and take the footpath round the 1st garden R to the next road (150m). Follow the lane R between fields and through a wood, past the wide side track R (350m) to the fork (150m). Fork L to the Vale houses (250m).

⑫ At the end of the track take the path up beside the gardens wall to the fields (150m). ✳ At the fork take any path (200m). Keep on ahead up the valley and L along the drive to the *Wotton Hatch* (500m) or, if returning to White Downs ascend to Wotton Church (50m). ➔①

23 Wotton, Broadmoor and Friday Street

About 7km/4½ miles with an extension of 1½ km/1 mile; mainly wooded valleys; several short steep slopes. OS 1:25000 146 Dorking,1:50000 187 Dorking.

Start from the village car park behind the *Wotton Hatch*, TQ 125 476, or from Broadmoor car park, TQ 132 454 (not on the side lane with the hamlet).

The Stephan Langton 01306 730775
The Wotton Hatch 01306 887694

21✿ 22✳ 27❖ 34★ 35✿

① Opposite the **Wotton Hatch**, take the drive to Wotton Church (300m) and enter the churchyard.

ⓔ *Extension of 1½km/1 mile: Exit L of the church and follow the path between fields down into the wood (250m). Stay ahead to the bottom of the wood (300m)* Guildford *and over a field to the track junction near houses (100m).*✳★

ⓕ *Turn back R on the valley track passing a house (500m).* ✿

ⓖ *After the house (100m) watch out for the cross path and go R up over the ridge and down to the Vale houses (200m). Keep on to the top end of the track then take the path up beside the garden wall to the fields (150m). At the fork take the lesser path L of the main path to the first pond (100m).* →③

② Exit R of the church on the path into the valley (50m). Turn L and fork R on the lesser path down to the second pond (150m).

③ Opposite the pond take the steep side path up the valleyside. Over the brow, cross the field on top towards the corner of the wood (250m). Cross the road and follow the track opposite, L of the wood (350m). At the farm drive continue, slightly L, on the footpath outside the fields under trees to end at a byway L (200m).

Dorking

The Rookery

Pipp Brook

1 mile

1 km

START

The Wotton Hatch

A25

WOTTON

RoW

GW

Wotton House

Sheephouse Lane

Tilling Bourne

N
W ☆ E
S

FRIDAY STREET

weir

Home Farm

The Stephan Langton

fb

BRO MOO

Leith Hill

ABINGER BOTTOM

alt START

46

© Crown Copyright MC 100011861

④ Past the byway take the drive L (50m) then diverge L on the track. Stay on the same track up the Tilling valley, below fields (1000m) then wood, past a house (250m) to Broadmoor hamlet (700m). ❖ Walk up the road to the last house (250m) and on, briefly (50m).

⑤ Turn R up the path beside the last garden. ✿ Go straight up steeply and across the ridge to the Broadmoor car park (200m).

⑥ From the vehicle entrance of the car park cross the road to the track junction behind the trees (20m) and turn L on the track parallel with the road (70m). Take the next side path R away from the road to the T-junction over the brow of the hill (250m). Turn L into the dip (40m) then R down the valley path (150m). Near the bottom fork L (20m) and keep going to the footbridge (100m). Cross it.

⑦ Walk down the track R to the road in Friday Street (150m). Stay ahead past the **Stephan Langton** (60m) to the road junction at the end of the pond (200m).

⑧ Opposite the corner of the pond go down the tarmac drive past the house. Stay ahead past a stone bridge L (450m), past a path diverging up R (450m) to the R bend (350m).

⑨ Just round the bend (30m) go L out of the trees (40m) and up the edge of the field to the drive (50m).

⑩ Walk down the drive L (100m). At the corner of the garden of Wotton House L (home of John Evelyn the diarist) turn R into cottage drive and bear slightly L up the field to the wood. Cross the wood and field to the A25 (350m).

⑪ Cross the road to path hidden behind the hedge and follow it R to the *Wotton Hatch* (400m).

John Evelyn (1620-1706) lived at Wotton House when not in London and wrote a diary of far more general interest than his contemporary, Pepys.   Extracts:

2/9/1666 This fatal night about ten, began that deplorable fire, neere Fishstreete in Lond: ... God grant mine eyes never to behold the like , who now saw above ten thousand houses all in one Flame   4/9/1666 The burning still rages .... It pleased his Majestie to command me among the rest to looke after the quenching of fetter-lane.

1/3/1671 I both saw and heard a very familiar discourse between the King and Mrs Nellie [Gwyn] ... I was heartily sorry at this scene: Thence the King walked to the Dutches of Cleavelands, another Lady of Pleasure & curse of our nation:

9/1/1684 I went crosse the Thames upon the Ice which was being quite frozen up ... incredibly thick, as to beare not onely whole streets of boothes in which the[y] roasted meate, & had divers shops of wares: 24/1/1684 The frost still continuing more & more severe ... 30/1/1684 .... & all manner of sports continuing & increasing: miserable were the wants of poore people, Deare universaly perished in most of the parks thro-out England, & very much Cattell:

22/10/1684 Sir William Godolphin and I went to see the Rhinocerous (or Unicorne) being the first that I suppose was ever brought into England: It more ressembled a huge enormous swine than any other Beast among us:

22/4/1708 ... went to the meeting of the R.Society ... I also saw Sir Isaac Newtons (now made knight at the Queenes entertaining at Oxon) 17/6/08 the burning glass ... which did strange things as to mealting whatever was held to it ... The Glasse was composed of 7 round burning glasses of about a foote diameter ...

The Diary of John Evelyn edited by Guy de la Bédoyère 1995 Boydell Press 380pp

24 Forest Green and Ewhurst

About 9 km/5½ miles; the short cut of 1km/¾ mile misses Ewhurst; undulating farmland; long views. OS maps 1:25000 146 Dorking, 1:50000 187 Dorking.

Start at Forest Green. Park on one of the village green tracks near the church, TQ 120 413. Ewhurst car park is near the route, TQ 091 403.

Linking walks 26✳ 30❖ (37)✳

The Bulls Head ☎ 01483 277447
The Parrot ☎ 01306 621339

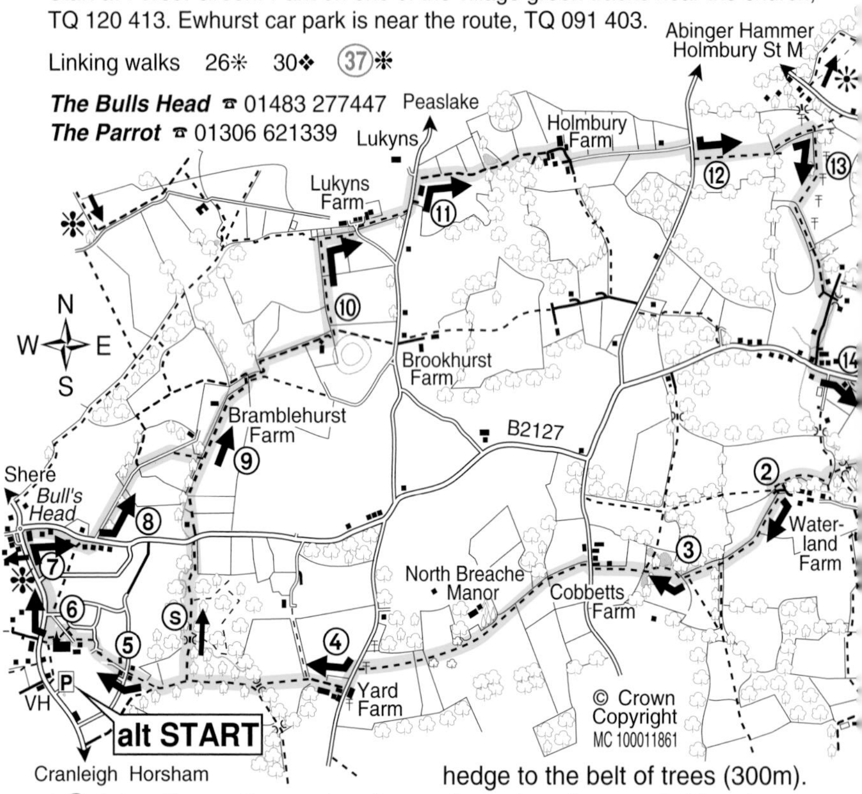

❖① Near Forest Green church, walk along the path on the narrow green to the wide part of the green. From here follow the vehicle track round the end house to the L bend (150m) and enter the field set back R between buildings. Go along the R fence into the trees (200m) and over the footbridge to the next field (30m). Turn L and follow the tree-lined edge (150m).

② Soon after the farm track L over the bridge (40m) turn L through the hedge. Cross the end of the narrow field (20m) and turn R along the hedge outside it. Stay with this hedge to the belt of trees (300m). Go up into the next field and on near the R edge (150m).

③ In the next field follow the edge R round to the pond (70m) and on (70m) then turn R between ponds into the next field (30m). Walk straight up past the hedge bend and along the hedge to the road at Cobbetts Farm (200m). Continue on the path opposite at the R edge of the fields up past North Breache Manor (450m). Carry on from gate to gate in subsequent fields. Keep to the same line diverging from the wood far R to meet the road 100m R of Yard Farm (450m).

④ Go L along the road (80m) and R on the path at the barns. Stay ahead between fields into the trees and over the stream to a path junction (300m). Keep on (R) to the side path at the next field R (250m).

Ⓢ *Short cut of 1km/¾ mile missing Ewhurst: Turn R on the side path then stay ahead: over the bridge (140m), through the wood (250m), between fields (100m), over the road, along the drive opposite, R of the house and along the L edge of fields beside the trees (300m). ➼⑨*

⑤ Continue ahead to Ewhurst, soon beside gardens (120m). Fork R up beside fields (100m). Cross the road and go up the drive opposite to the garden gate (70m) then diverge R on the footpath between gardens to the next road (50m). Go down the road (40m) and take the path L between houses. At the end turn L across a drive to the churchyard (120m). Pass R of the church to the village street (100m).

⑥ Follow the pavement R to the road junction at the little green and the **Bulls Head** (400m). ✳

⑦ Turn R along the pavement of Ockley Road. Watch out L for the drive of Bramblehurst Farm (250m).

⑧ Follow the drive between fields and round a R bend (300m). Watch out for a side path R, ²/₃ of the way to the L bend (150m). Cross the field ½L and the stream in the trees to the next field (100m). Turn L.

⑨ Stay beside the trees to the end of the field (300m). Turn L but don't enter the field ahead. Take the path R along the hedge (70m). Stay with the hedge round L & R bends and up, L of the house, into the field with the hillock (300m).

⑩ Turn L along the edge away from the hillock and keep on to the fences of Lukyns Farm (300m). Turn R up the fence to the tarmac drive (150m). Cross the drive slightly L and continue outside the field at the edge of the Lukyns garden to the road (200m).

⑪ Go L up the road (100m). Just before Lukyns drive L, take the track R down beside fields, past a pond L (300m) and ahead up to Holmbury Farm (250m). At the barn L turn R on the main track (50m). At the farm house, turn L down the tarmac drive to the road (450m).

⑫ Turn R along the road (40m) and take the path L across the middle of the field (300m). At the far edge continue in the L field at the R edge to the end hedge of the adjacent field R (180m). ✳

⑬ At the 4-way path junction turn R into the corner of the side field and follow the R hedge (150m). Bear R round the end of the hedge over to the nearest part of the edge and into the next field (150m). Follow the path L near the edge and stay ahead down the track past a house L to the unmade road with more houses (350m).

⑭ Follow this drive R to the road (250m). Cross and go L along the verge (100m), When the green broadens bear R on the path to the church (100m).

Leith Hill

START

P

Ockley
A29

The Parrot
VH

FOREST GREEN
①

25 Leith Hill and Holmbury Hill

About 9½ km/6 miles with an extension of 400m/¼ mile; a Lower Greensand walk; hilly woodland. OS maps 1:25000 146 Dorking 1:50000 187 Dorking.

Start from Starveall Corner car park on Leith Hill, TQ 130 432, or a roadside parking spot on the B2126 in Holmbury near Pasture Wood Road, TQ 112 440.

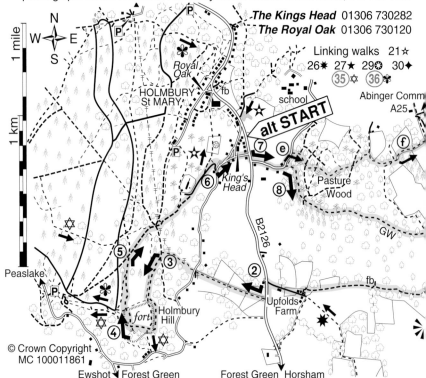

The Kings Head 01306 730282
The Royal Oak 01306 730120

Linking walks 21★
26✳ 27★ 29◉ 30◆
㉟✿ ㊱✿

✳① From Starveall Corner car park turn L along the road (100m) and take the side track R at the end of the wide layby. Stay ahead, winding down to a house drive (500m). Still ahead, carry on down through the wood, over a foot-bridge (600m), beside fields and eventually round a L bend into Upfolds Farmyard (550m). Turn R along the drive to the road (250m).

② Go on the road L (100m) and turn into the field R. Follow the path up the R hedge to the next road (400m). Cross and go straight up the flank of Holmbury Hill (250m).

③ At the wide track turn L (30m) then fork R up the side path. Stay on the edge of Holmbury Hill, into a dip and on beside the hillfort (500m). Go round the corner of the hill R and on to the Bray memorial seat and view point down L (150m).

④ Go back up to the summit. ✿✿ Follow the main track away from the edge of the escarpment across the fort ramparts (150m) and on to the oblique cross track (300m).

⑤ Bear R to the 5-way junction (350m) and stay ahead, past the end of the cricket field L (400m), to the track fork (100m). ★

⑥ Keep to the main track, down R round a R bend to the road in Holmbury St Mary (200m). Walk down the road L (40m). Fork R to the main road at the bottom (250m) (or L for the **Kings Head**).

⑦ Turn R beside the main road (60m) then L up Pasture Wood Road to the L bend (250m).

⑨ *Just down the road (20m) take the forest track on the other side. Disregard side paths L (150m) and continue up to the fork (400m)*

⑨ *Bear L then stay ahead up to the tower on the summit of Leith Hill (900m). Turn R.* ➔⑪

⑧ On the bend go straight up the woodland path. Stay ahead up the winding and undulating edge of the hill to High Ash Farm (1400m). Follow the curving drive out R to the track T-junction (150m).

⑨ Turn L up to the road (120m) and back R on the road (40m) then take the track L winding R & L up between old Hythe Sandstone quarries to the long straight path which slopes down L (250m).

⑩ Turn L (40m) then R on the oblique cross track. Stay ahead in a straight line to the Greensand Way track on the edge of Leith Hill (850m) with summit tower visible L. Walk up to the tower (200m) ✪ then return.

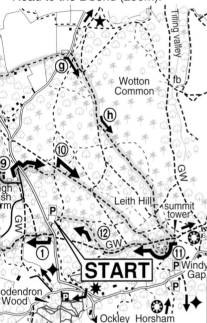

↖↗ Northwards are two shoulders of the North Downs with Dorking in the Mole Gap: Ranmore Common, L with the church spire and Box Hill, R. Southwards are the South Downs.

⑪ From the tower walk down the track on the edge of the hill, the Greensand Way (50m) and take the first gravel path L (signposted to Windy Gap car park) (70m). ✦ Don't drop down the steep path L to the car park but continue round the hillock back to the GW track (150m). Follow this track or the footpath beside it down the edge of the escarpment (400m).

⑫ After the S-bend bear R on the side path (200m) to the cross path then L down to the car park (150m).

ⓔ *Extension of 400m/¼ mile: Continue round the bend (100m) then take the path R into Pasture Wood. Stay ahead up the winding path to a field corner (650m). Bear R to the next corner (50m) and keep on to the next field (150m).*

ⓕ *Follow the R edge (150m) and stay ahead: outside the next field (100m), over a bridleway, over the road (40m), down to the valley path (100m), up through the wood past houses R (250m), straight across the field down into the corner of the wood (120m) and up the edge to the next road (200m).* ★

26 Starveall Corner, Forest Green and Upfolds

About 7½ km/4¾ miles with an extension of 3 km/2 miles; hilly farmland and woods on Wealden Clay. OS maps 1:25000 146 Dorking, 1:50000 187 Dorking.

Start at Starveall Corner car park, TQ 130 432, or at the Forest Green kerbside.

Linking 24✳ 25✹ 27☆ 29✿ 30✳

The Parrot ☎ 01306 621339

② Go L down the road (70m) and turn R to the gate of the Rhododendron Wood (30m). Go straight down (50m) and take the 1st side path R (150m). After the car park, descend L (30m) and take the winding path, 1st R (200m). Near the end descend L,R to the track (from the road) outside fields (50m). Pass R of the top fence (20m) to enter the field L.

③ Go down the L edge of the fields to the wood (200m), obliquely across the wood (100m) and the next field to the far L corner (120m), into the next field (20m) then down the L edge to the road (700m).

④ Turn R along the road (80m) then cross to the green. Follow the path near the L edge to the **Parrot** in Forest Green village (300m).

⑤ Bear R across the village green, L of the cricket field, towards the bungalow (200m). Go L along the winding concrete drive, over a bridge (350m) to side tracks (30m).

✿☆✳① Go up the path at the top of Starveall Corner car park (50m) & R on the cross path down to the track (150m). Keep on L of the road until the path joins the road (400m).

52

(e) *Extension of 3km/2 miles:*
Turn L along the track to the fields.
Go round the R bend (100m). At
the L bend enter the field ahead
(20m) and turn L along the edge.
Cross into Field 2 and keep on in
the same direction past the narrow
end of the wood (300m). In the
field ahead follow the R hedge
(150m). Cross Field 4 to the far L
corner and Field 5 along the L
end to Bridgham Farm (120m).

(f) *Turn R on the bridleway*
between fields. Keep on round
bends LRL up to houses (450m).

(g) *Stay ahead on the tarmac lane*
round R to the L bend (80m) then
take the side path ahead (150m).
When it ends at the fields turn R
under the trees. Keep on between
fields (500m) and into the narrow
elongated field. Stay ahead to the
far R corner (200m) and through
the belt of trees to the next field
(50m). Diverge from the R edge
down to the far L corner (200m).
Climb to the next field (20m). Go R
round the edge to the pond (70m)
and on (70m) then turn R between
ponds to the next field (30m). ✳

(h) *Don't enter this field but turn R*
on the side path past another pond
to another field (80m). Go straight
across into the corner (120m).

(i) *Turn R along the adjacent field.*
Keep to the L edge (200m). In the
next fields, identify the far L corner
in the trees then cross ahead to
the R edge and follow it round to
the far L corner (550m). ♦(7)

(6) Turn R into the trees. Follow
the path near the stream (150m).
At the bridge R turn L into the field
(30m). Go R round the edge to the
stile in the corner (150m).

(7) Cross the fence and stream to
the garden. Go up to the drive and
ahead to the road (150m). Turn L
along the verge (50m) then cross
and walk along Mill Lane (250m).

(8) Just before crossing a bridge
turn L on the track beside the
stream (200m). At the field keep on
up the R edge (150m) then turn R
to the path in the side field. Cross
to the nearest trees (100m). Pass
R of them along the hedge into the
corner (150m). Cross the next field
slightly L to the footbridge (70m)
and go on between gardens to the
road (80m). Slightly L enter the field
opposite. The exit is 50m R of the
far L corner. The right of way is at
the edge but there is usually a
direct path over the rise (200m).

(9) Continue ahead across the end
of the next field (70m) and turn L
into the next. Follow the L edge to
the top corner and go through the
belt of trees (250m). Turn L over to
the next wood and go up through
that (100m) then up the R edge of
the next field to the corner of the
wood (100m). Bear L over the field.
Aim for the lowest spot with Upfolds
Farm beyond and cross to the gate
(300m). Continue on the track
ahead through the farm (50m).✳

(10) After the L barn turn R between
the buildings (50m). Pass round a
R bend and keep on between the
wood L and field R (450m). Cross a
stream and go on up to the broad
track near a house R (550m).

(11) Opposite, bear R up the steeper
track. Stay on this winding track up
to the field (250m) then beside the
field and on up to the road (200m).
Turn L (50m) and cut through the
trees R to the car park (50m).

27 Friday Street, Coldharbour and Leith Hill

About 9km/5¾ miles with a short cut of 700m/½ mile omitting Coldharbour and *The Plough*; woodland, heath and the highest hill in Surrey. Long ascents, one very steep but short. OS maps 1:25000 146 Dorking 1:50000 187 Dorking.

Start from the National Trust (free) car park near Friday Street, TQ 125 457. Several car parks on Leith Hill are near the walk eg Windy Gap, TQ 139 429.

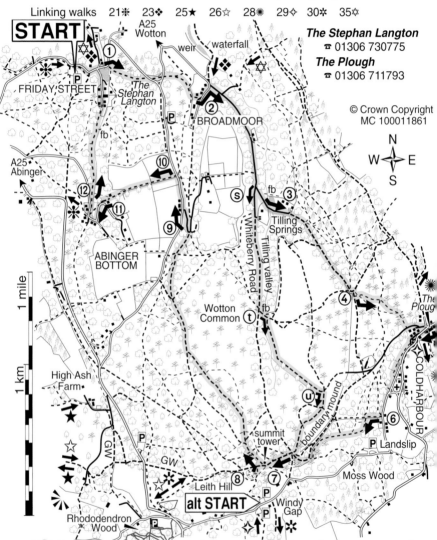

Linking walks 21✳ 23❖ 25★ 26☆ 28✹ 29✧ 30✺ 35✵

The Stephan Langton
☎ 01306 730775

The Plough
☎ 01306 711793

© Crown Copyright
MC 100011861

❖① From Friday Street car park go down the path beside the road then down the road and across the end of the pond (250m). After the pond turn R up the steep oblique path under trees to the same road (300m). Cross obliquely and go on over the next road (50m) to the path fork (100m). Bear R then turn R to pass above gardens (250m.)

② Turn L down the side path between gardens into Broadmoor (50m). Walk down the road L to the bend (70m) ✿ and turn R on the 1st hard track. Pass a side track L (100m) and a cottage L (350m) and keep on up to a track fork (300m).

Ⓢ *Short cut of 1km/¾ mile: Fork R (200m). After the house drive L continue up the Tilling valley to the the oblique cross path (600m).*

Ⓣ *Turn L (30m), cross the infant Tillingbourne (20m) and take the next track R. The bourne shrinks to a boggy area at the highest spring (700m). Continue up to the 4-way track junction on the ridge (100m).*

Ⓤ *Turn R. Stay on the undulating track, eventually down to a 5-way junction in a cleft (500m). ➔⑦*

③ Fork L (100m). Stay ahead R of the pond and garden, up past a house drive L and a converging track R (300m) to the S-bend with side tracks R & L (350m).

④ Go on a bit up the valley but after the L side track (20m) take the little side path L up the side to a cross path on top (200m). Bear R over it then stay on this path over cross paths on the end of the hill down to a cart track (300m). Descend L to the **Plough** in Coldharbour (150m). ❋✧

⑤ Turn R through the village (60m) and bear R up the track with houses. Keep on, curving L round the trees. Just before the road take the onward footpath above the road almost to the church (250m). Carry on along the road (300m).

⑥ At the next garden R take the steep path straight up (60m). Just over the brow turn L on the wide cross path. Follow it around the

edge of the hill until it bends through the boundary mound to a wide track (500m). Go L down the track, round a R bend, to the 5-way junction in the cleft (150m).

⑦ From the cleft in the hill go up the track on the other side to the summit tower of Leith Hill (200m) (north view R from the tower, south view L 50m after it). ★☆❋

◤◥ To the north are the North Downs with Dorking in the notch cut by the River Mole. Box Hill is R of the gap and Ranmore Common with the church spire L of the gap. Southwards the distant ridge is the South Downs.

⑧ Take the side path nearest the tower away from the edge of the hill through a complex of cross paths to a fork (200m). Bear R and keep to the path on the brow above the valley R, gently downwards (750m). Join a converging track and carry on, sinking into a valley. Stay ahead to join the farm track on the hairpin bend (850m).

⑨ Bear L up the farm track to the road at Wotton Barn (150m). Walk down the road R, past the houses and the narrow field L (200m).

⑩ Turn L into the corner of the next field. Continue at the L edge until part way down the 2nd field then bear L to houses and drop to the drive (500m).

⑪ Stay ahead up the drive (50m) and down the winding road into Abinger Bottom hamlet (300m). ❋ Continue on the straight (50m).

⑫ At the last house, bear R down the track beside the stream to the road in Friday Street (650m). Keep on past the **Stephan Langton** to the end of the pond (300m). For the car park go L up the road then up the path above the road (200m).

28 Holmwood Common and Coldharbour

About 9 km/5½ miles with a short cut of 500m and an extension of 1 km/¾ mile; farmland and forest; short steep slopes; fine views; several stiles; bluebells in season. OS maps 1:25000 146 Dorking, 1:50000 187 Dorking.

Start at South Holmwood from Mill Road car park, TQ 172 451.

The Plough ☏ 01306 711793   Linking walks 27 ✳   29 ★   44 ✦

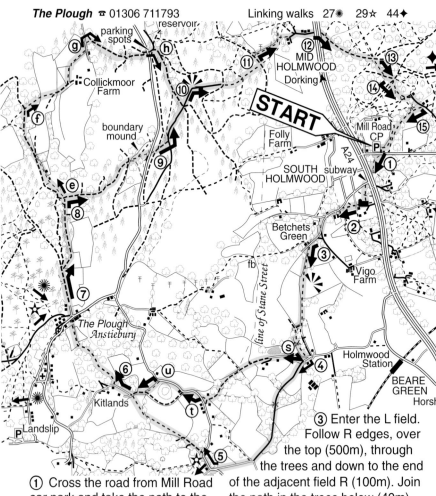

① Cross the road from Mill Road car park and take the path to the war memorial (130m). Go under the A24 (50m), R on the side road (20m) & L up to the church (100m).
② Go R behind the church, out at the gate and ahead down to the pond (150m). Walk up the road L, round L & R curves past Betchets Green to East Lodge (300m).

③ Enter the L field. Follow R edges, over the top (500m), through the trees and down to the end of the adjacent field R (100m). Join the path in the trees below (40m) and go L to the lane (200m). ★ ✳

ⓢ *Short cut of 500m: Turn R up the lane (200m). After the houses L stay ahead on the track over the rise up, down, up to a fork between houses (600m). Ascend R (50m).*
ⓣ *Go up the winding road R, past the lodge L (150m) and on (200m).*

56

(u) *After the hillock L watch out for the path in the field with the hillock. Go down the R edge (100m) and bear R along the track (100m).* ➤(6)

(4) Turn L (50m) then R back down the drive. Stay ahead on the track between fields (800m) and (R) along the tarmac drive (300m).

(5) Walk up the road R (150m). On the R bend take the track L under trees into the field (150m). Diverge slightly from the L edge up the foot of the slope to the stile and footbridge halfway up the end fence (300m). Cross to the next field and turn R, diverging from the fence, up the steepest part to the field gate under trees at the top (200m).

(6) Walk up the drive (150m). On the L bend take the path R up through the wood (400m). Stay ahead through the field up the R edge then between gardens to the road in Coldharbour (200m).

(7) Opposite the **Plough** go down the drive beside the field and on along the forest track (300m). At the end of the field, turn R down the first side track which bends L outside another field (100m). Carry on to the cross track (400m).

(e) *Extension of 1 km/¾ mile: Stay ahead on the L small path past a shed and house (200m), outside fields (100m), then on the track in the trees to the cross path (300m).*

(f) *Turn R down to the field (150m) and descend towards the farm (200m). Turn L into the field before the farmyard and follow R edges to the farm drive in the trees (250m)*

(g) *Go L up the drive, watching out for the path R (60m). Turn R up the path (20m) and R up the track, ever upwards to the road (450m).*

(h) *Go up the track opposite (50m) and take the side track, curving R. Stay on this track to the 5-way junction (450m). Turn L.* ➤(10)

(8) Turn R down into the valley (100m) and go straight up the other side curving L and R over the brow to the cross track at the boundary mound (500m). Cross the mound ahead (20m) and bear L up the path (50m). Just after the bend bear R up the faint path to the road (50m) and join the path opposite.

(9) Carry on up to the forest track on the ridge (100m). Follow it L round the R curve and down through a 5-way junction (300m).

(10) Go down the edge of the spur ridge, past side tracks (350m), over the knoll (50m), steeply down to the cross path (70m) and down to the track around the foot (200m).

(11) Turn L (60m) then cross to the corner of the field R (20m). Follow the path R of the field (200m). Just round the bottom corner, turn R on the side path to houses (100m). Carry on down the drive then the unmade road to the A24 (200m).

(12) Cross to the path opposite and stay on it down through Holmwood Common and up to the complex junction on the summit (500m). ✦

(13) Bear R down the 2nd R path (100m) then L on the wide path to a major cross path (100m).

(14) Cross the tiny valley R and fork L to the side path L (30m). Follow it, avoiding R branches, to a house (150m). Go down the drive (100m).

(15) Opposite the next houses turn R on the hard path up through the wood (350m). Near the top transfer to the adjacent path R which bends R to Mill Road car park (150m).

29 Leith Hill and Buckinghill Farm

About 6½ km/4 miles with an extension of 1 km/¾ mile and cut of 800m/½ mile. Heath, woods and farmland; steep slopes; fine views. The lower parts are on the Wealden Clay. OS maps 1:25000 146 Dorking, 1:50000 187 Dorking.

Start at Leith Hill Windy Gap car park, TQ 139 428. Landslip car park, TQ 147 432, is on the route but is no good for the extension.

The Plough ☎ 01306 711793

Linking 25❂ 26✿
27✧ 28★ 30❀

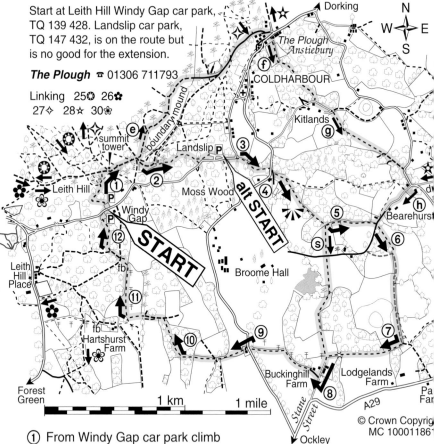

① From Windy Gap car park climb the stepped zigzag path (200m). ❂ Over the brow, cross ½R to the Leith Hill tower (150m).✧ Continue on the main track (Greensand Way) past the tower, soon descending to a 5-way junction in a cleft (200m).

ⓔ *Extension of 1km/¾ mile via Coldharbour: Take the L uphill track which winds and undulates past side tracks L (850m). After the cricket field, join the converging track (GW). Continue down to the* **Plough** *in Coldharbour (500m).* ★

ⓕ *Over the road take the path R of the house, between hedges (30m) then down the L edge of the field (150m) and on through the wood below Anstiebury Hill (400m). At the drive descend L to the field (150m).*

ⓖ *Aim halfway down the opposite fence where there is a footbridge (150m) and cross the next field to the far R corner beside the wood (300m). Join the onward track out of the field (150m) and go R down the road to the next bend (150m).*

ⓗ *Turn R up the Bearehurst drive (250m). Stay ahead on the farm track down to the bend in the dip (100m). Turn L into the field.* ➤⑥

② Take the R uphill track. Ignore the L fork almost immediately, and continue up curving L (150m). At the L bend on top take the side path R over the brow of the hill and down obliquely L. Stay on the path through Landslip car park (500m) then turn L up the road (100m).

③ At the road bend L take the path ahead in the trees R of the field down to the next road (300m). Go down the track opposite (30m) and turn L into the field (which has two diverging uphill paths).

④ Aim for the trees 50m after the paddocks at the R edge and pass through to the next field (100m). Cut across the L corner of the field to the protruding corner of wood (200m). Carry on beside it then through it to the next field (200m).

Ⓢ *Short cut of 800m/½ miles: Go straight down the fields. Aim for the gap between the wood L and the trees around the pond R (450m), crossing an estate road on the way. Go through the gap then follow the R edge of the wood (300m). Stay ahead over the field (170m).* ➤⑧

⑤ Turn L and follow the edge of the wood down through fields to the track in the trees at the bottom (370m). Go into the field opposite.

⑥ Cross obliquely to the end of the line of trees over the rise. If the path is unclear, take a bisecting line out of the corner (200m). Bear R past the trees then follow the edge of the field (150m) and turn R into the next adjacent large field. Keep on in the same direction R of the

hedge. The footpath crosses the hedge L just over the rise but it is easier to stay R of the hedge until the track bends L (450m).

⑦ Go R, along the bottom edge of the field to the corner at the wood (150m). Stay ahead beside the wood (300m), over a bridge in the belt of trees, to the next field and along the edge to the farm track L (100m). Turn L.

⑧ Go through Buckinghill Farm on the track (overlying Stane Street) (150m). After the stream turn back R on the side track past a house (100m). Stay ahead in the field round the R edge to the road opposite a house (450m).

⑨ Cross to the drive on the bend (30m) and pass through the garden to the field behind the house. Make for the bottom L corner (150m). Stay ahead though the trees, along the R edge of the next field (250m) and into the next wood (100m).

⑩ Just before the next field turn R on the path up through the wood to the track linking the fields (300m). Turn L up a little rise. Go on to the corner of the wood R (150m) and ahead over the field (100m). ❀❀

⑪ Halfway across turn R up the little depression in the field making for the corner of the wood at the L edge of the field higher up (200m). Keep on up the edge of the field to the top corner (200m) then enter the wood. Follow the path over the footbridge then up round to the tracks (80m).

⑫ Cross the main track and go up the side track to the bend (80m) then R up the side path to the road (300m). Windy Gap car park is R.

30 Leith Hill, Jayes Park and Forest Green

About 9¼km/5¾ miles with an extension of 1½ km/1 mile to Ockley and a short cut of of 3½ km/2¼ miles; hilly heath and farmland on the Lower Greensand escarpment. OS maps 1:25000 146 Dorking, 1:50000 187 Dorking.

Start at Windy Gap car park, Leith Hill, TQ 139 428, or at the roadside in Forest Green, TQ 123 412, or, on the extension, at Ockley cricket green, TQ 147 398.

Linking walks   24❖   25✦
26✳   27✸   29✿   31✳   32⊙

The Parrot 01306 621339
Inn on the Green 01306 711032

🐾① Just up the road from the Windy Gap car parks take the downhill track next to the house. Go round a R bend (350m) and down to the second junction which has two side tracks L (400m).

② Turn back L down the track through the trees (80m) and R on the 1st side track (150m). At the bottom of the slope pass between fields to the next wood and go on (300m). After the R bend (50m) are side paths R & L.

Ⓢ *Short cut of 3½km/2¼ miles: Stay ahead to the edge of the wood (100m) and over the track into the L field. Cross diagonally (200m) and go on along the hedge in the next field to the road (250m).*

ⓣ *Turn R. Soon after the drive of Etherley Farm (60m) turn L into the field. Keep to L edges (past a track L) to the end of the fields (400m). Continue through the wood to the forest track (200m). Turn R.* ✦⑪

③ Go L to the edge of the wood (200m), into the field, round the R corner (70m). Stay ahead down the edge, then under trees to the barn

(400m), along the track to the road (300m), over into the field opposite (30m) and across it on the unofficial path (150m).

④ Follow the Jayes Park drive past the farm buildings, round L & R bends and on, L of the barns

© Crown Copyright
MC 100011861

(250m). After the walled garden L, bear L between fields to the house (150m) and L again to the end of the track (60m). Carry on ahead down the field to the cross path, 50m before the wood (200m).

ⓔ *Extension of 1½ km/1 mile: Go L across the adjacent field, over the footbridge (120m), round the corner of the wood (50m) to the next corner (150m) ◐ then stay ahead past the house at the gap in the trees to Ockley village green (250m). ✽ (The Inn is above 80m).*

ⓕ *Turn R past the cricket pitch to the corner (300m), R down the track (100m) and R across the bridge and cemetery to the field (50m). Go L at the edge, over to the corner (200m). Outside follow the bridleway L, winding between fields and trees to the road (600m).*

ⓖ *Follow the road R (400m). ♦ⓖ*

⑤ Turn R to the far corner of the field (400m). Cross the bridge to the corner of the next field and follow the path outside it in the trees (150m). Cross the road.

⑥ Go up the Volvens Farm drive (200m). After the buildings, pass R of the little field, across the gravel drive, along the R hedge and into the field R (100m). Follow the L edge round the corner (40m) and past the cottage (100m).

⑦ Stay ahead on the farm drive (30m), round the L bend and down past the pond and farm house (150m). Pass round a slight L bend (500m). At the next L bend (150m) watch out for the side path R in the trees.

⑧ Take the side path R over the stream to the field (50m). ❖✳ Go along the R edge of the fields to a narrow end (200m) and carry on at the L edge of the next field. Bear L across the garden then follow the track briefly and cross the grass L to the road in Forest Green (250m). Turn R along the road (150m).

⑨ After the **Parrot** bear R across the grass verge beside the trees to re-join the road after the R bend (300m). Follow the road round the bend to the wood L (80m).

⑩ Just into the wood (50m) take the side path ahead, winding uphill to a 3-way junction (350m). Turn R to the cart track (80m) and stay ahead round the L bend (70m).

⑪ Keep on up round the S-bend to the next R bend (200m) then bear L on the side path up to the junction at the edge of the wood (250m) ✦

⑫ Go up the edge (200m). Level with the top of the field (50m before the road) turn R (30m) then L up into Rhododendron Wood. Avoid side paths R (200m). At the 1st cross path turn L (30m). Cross car park obliquely then go over the grass to the far top corner (150m).

⑬ Go out to the road between junctions (30m). Cross the main road and turn L beside it (70m). Opposite the side road bear R on the path (30m) then fork R up the steeper path beside the wall (80m). Pass round the R bend and carry on up to the track (300m). Turn R up to Leith Hill tower (500m). ✽

⑭ 50m before the tower, turn R on the side path. Go round the little hillock (100m) and drop down the stepped path to Windy Gap (200m).

31 Ockley, Jayes Park and Vann Lake

About 9 km/ 5½ miles with a short cut of 3 km/2 miles and an extension of 2½ km/1½ miles. Barely undulating farmland and woodland on Wealden Clay. OS maps 1:25000 146 Dorking+134 Crawley, 1:50000 185 Dorking.

Start at Ockley village green from the Cricket car park, TQ 147 398.

The Inn on the Green ☎ 01306 711032 **The Kings Arms** ☎ 01306 711224
The Cricketers Arms ☎ 01306 627205 Linking walks 30❊ 32◇

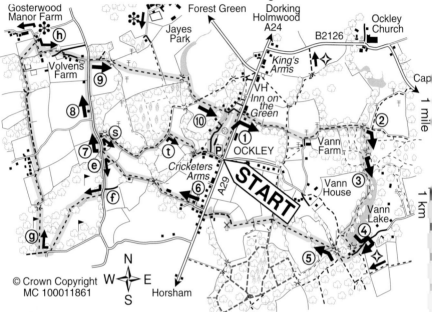

© Crown Copyright
MC 100011861

① From Ockley cricket pavilion walk along the path near the road (Stane Street) to the house drive just before the **Inn on the Green** (350m). (The **Kings Arms** is 300m further along the road). Cross the road and go up the path between gardens. Stay ahead to the field (150m) and up the R edge to the end of the trees (200m). ◇ Cross the field ahead aiming slightly R to the gate after the farmhouse below (150m). Don't go through but carry on round the field to the gate R into the trees (200m). Follow the bridleway through the trees (100m). After the field R use the upper path and descend into the gill (200m).

② Just after the bridge (20m) take the small side path R. Watch out for a path and footbridge R (150m).
③ Re-cross the gill up to the path on the brow (50m). Follow it L between Vann Lake L and fields R to the path T-junction at the end of the lake (550m).
④ Turn L across the end of the lake and ascend to a vehicle track (200m). Go R down the track past houses (100m) and continue L of the garden to the junction (100m).
⑤ Turn R down to the bridge and up to the next path junction (60m). Turn L to the field (20m). Take a bisecting line out of the corner to cross the opposite edge at the mid

62

point (200m). Keep on in the same line through the far L corner (200m) and over more fields, up to the windmill (400m). Go R on the track down past Elmers Farm and up to the main road in Ockley (250m).

⑥ Cross the road slightly R and go up Elmers Road opposite. Stay ahead to the field (150m). Go down the L edge beside the wood (200m), round a slight bend into the gill (60m) over the bridge and up into the field (20m). Carry on up the L edge past a house L (200m). In the next field follow the hedge R to the corner (100m). Cross the next field obliquely to the house (120m) and join the road. ✤

ⓔ *Extension of 2½ km/1½ mile: Walk L along the road past the drive of Parklands Farm (300m).*

ⓕ *Just after it (40m) take the path R through the trees to the golf course (60m). Stay ahead beside trees (60m), round, R of, the pond (60m) and on beside the belt of trees (80m). Turn L at the gap in the trees (20m) and cross the fairways ½R to the far edge (200m). Join the path through the trees to the tarmac drive (80m).*

ⓖ *Turn R (20m). Don't go round the L bend but stay ahead on the track watching out for the side path R (80m). Go through the trees to the golf course (50m), straight over past the R end of the belt of trees and down to the footbridge in the valley (250m). Cross to the field and go up the R edge (200m). At the hedge corner near the farm enter the adjacent field R. Cross the L corner to the next field (40m) and follow the R edge to the road (80m). In the field opposite carry*

on at the L edge eventually curving R to the corner of the tree lined hedge (400m). Where the track bends L down to another field go up into the trees and along the edge of the next field (150m), past a wall R and into the next field (100m). Ascend obliquely across the middle, aiming for the R edge of the house above (120m).

ⓗ *Cross the hedge and turn R beside it (80m). Go L round the corner (40m) then R into the trees. Follow the path L (80m). Cross the drive obliquely to Volvens Farm and go down the drive to the road (200m). Continue opposite.* ➜⑨

⑦ *Go R to the next house (100m).*

ⓢ *Short cut of 3 km/2 miles: At the house, take the bridleway R, winding around fields and beside a wood L to the gate R in the first corner of the last field (600m).*

ⓣ *Turn R. Diverge from the R edge into the far corner (200m). Go R across the cemetery and bridge then L to the green (150m).*

⑧ Stay on the road R past wood R (250m) and fields R to the drive of Volvens Farm (250m). Turn R.

⑨ Follow the path inside the edge of the wood and cross the bridge (200m). Bear R on the path across the foot of the slope at Jayes Park converging very gradually on the wood R. Stay ahead over the foot bridge and past the pond L at the corner of the wood (550m).

⑩ Go round the corner and down the edge to the next corner (150m). Aim for the house at the gap in the trees (200m). Join the drive across the end of the pond to the village green (20m) and go round R or across to the parking area (400m).

32 Capel, Vann Lake and Ockley Church

About 9½ km/6 miles with an extension of 1 km/¾ mile; gently undulating farmland and woods; on the Wealden Clay but mainly on farm drives.
OS maps 1:25000 146 Dorking+134 Crawley, 1:50000 187 Dorking.

Start at Capel village hall, TQ 176 408 or, on the extension, at Ockley green TQ 147 398.

Linking walks   30✪   31✧   33☆

The Crown 01306 711130
The Inn on the Green 01306 711032
The Kings Arms 01306 711224

① At Capel Memorial Hall walk onto the sports field and cut across the R corner to pass L of the bowling green hedge (200m). Take the path between gardens to the road (50m). Cross (20m R) to the field opposite. Make for the far L corner (80m) and go out, over a bridge, and round past the stables to the fields (40m). Walk up the R edge (200m) and ahead through the thicket with R & L bends to a T-junction (250m). Turn L (20m) and follow the main path round the R bend. Keep on to the side path at the trig point in the hedge (300m).
② Turn L down into the wood (150m). Stay ahead, across a track and gill at the far edge (150m) and along the R edge of the field to Pleystowe Farm (200m),
③ Follow the track R past barns (100m) then bear R on the drive to the road (150m). Cross slightly L (30m) and follow the path between fields to a footbridge near houses (500m). Cross and pass between gardens to the rough road (50m). Turn R to the main road (70m).
④ Follow the pavement L to the start of the trees R (200m) then take the farm drive R, which winds down under the railway (300m) to Osbrooks (350m). Keep on through

the farm and along the track between fields (400m).
⑤ Turn R down the next farm drive to the road (600m). Cross into the field opposite and follow the R edge round to the corner (150m).
⑥ Cross the next field diagonally (100m) and go on along the bottom field edges to the wood (400m). ✧
⑦ Follow the path into the wood, up the R edge (100m) and round a bend ½L to the house (60m).
⑧ Go up the drive R (50m) and take the descending side path. Cross the end of Vann Lake to the path between fields (200m) and

middle of the field slightly R to the trees at the top (300m). Go on through the trees into the next field (20m). Turn L. ➔⑩

⑨ Turn R through the trees to fields. Follow L edges to the end of the wood (350m) and go straight over to the far edge (150m). Don't go into the trees here but R.

⑩ Follow the edge of the trees (50m) then cross through the trees into the field below. Go down the L edge, round the corner R to the gateway (200m) then across the adjacent field to the road (200m).

⑪ Follow the road R to Ockley Church (400m). Carry on round the twists to the next R bend (150m).

⑫ Branch off ahead on the farm drive, between fields (400m) then beside a wood (200m). When the drive curves L to the house take the path ahead over the field and up with the rising hedges to the railway bridge (200m). Carry on ahead and cross the A24 (150m). Find the way into the field ahead (not the path outside the L edge). Make for the gap in the trees (200m). Cross the next field ahead down to the end of the converging fence (200m). ☆

⑬ Cross the next little field to the R corner (not to the stile near the fenced pond) (60m). Go up the next field to the top L corner (200m). Ditto the next field (150m). Outside it turn L (R of hedge) to the church-yard. Pass R of the church to the road next to the **Crown** (200m).

⑭ Walk along the road L to the Memorial Hall car park (150m).

follow it R up past Vann House R (400m). Carry on up the drive to the cross path in the trees just after the house R on the ridge (250m).

ⓔ *Extension of 1 km/¾ mile: Continue on the road down to the A29 Stane Street in Ockley (400m).*

ⓕ *Cross to the parking area.* ✪ *Go down (100m) round the edge of the village green past the pond (300m). (The drive R leads up to the **Inn on the Green**). Carry on at the L edge of the green past the house frontages and bear R up to the village hall (with Dutch gables) at the road junction (350m).*

ⓖ *Cross the main road. Take the path L of the village hall and up the*

33 Capel and Newdigate

About 9 km/5¾ miles with a short cut of 1 km/¾ mile; farmland and woods on the Wealden Clay; lots of stiles; gently undulating; half shady.
OS maps 1:25000 146 Dorking, 1:50000 187 Dorking.

Start at Capel village hall, TQ 178 408 or Newdigate village hall, TQ 196 422.

The Crown ☎ 01306 711130
The Six Bells ☎ 01306 631276

Linking walk   32☆

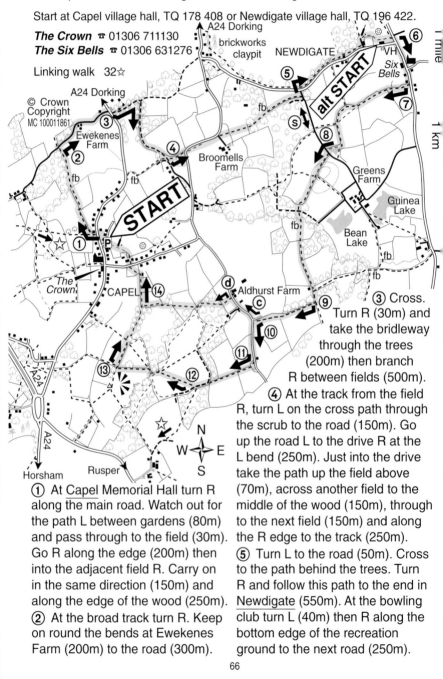

③ Cross. Turn R (30m) and take the bridleway through the trees (200m) then branch R between fields (500m).

④ At the track from the field R, turn L on the cross path through the scrub to the road (150m). Go up the road L to the drive R at the L bend (250m). Just into the drive take the path up the field above (70m), across another field to the middle of the wood (150m), through to the next field (150m) and along the R edge to the track (250m).

⑤ Turn L to the road (50m). Cross to the path behind the trees. Turn R and follow this path to the end in Newdigate (550m). At the bowling club turn L (40m) then R along the bottom edge of the recreation ground to the next road (250m).

① At Capel Memorial Hall turn R along the main road. Watch out for the path L between gardens (80m) and pass through to the field (30m). Go R along the edge (200m) then into the adjacent field R. Carry on in the same direction (150m) and along the edge of the wood (250m).

② At the broad track turn R. Keep on round the bends at Ewekenes Farm (200m) to the road (300m).

⑥ Walk down the road R past the church L and **Six Bells** R (200m) to the first field R (120m). Turn R.

⑦ Follow the R hedge around the fields, past side paths over the ditch, to a banked pond R (750m).

⑧ Pass R of the pond to the farm track (100m) and, slightly L, go up the L edge of the field opposite over the knoll (200m) and down to the wood (250m). Cross the belt of trees and the track to the foot bridge and the next field (100m). Go straight over to the R corner of the L wood (100m), through the edge of the wood (150m) and up the R edge of the field (200m). Pass a house in the trees R and keep on in the next field (100m).

⑨ Enter the adjacent field R and follow the edge to the road (900m).

ⓒ *Short cut of 1 km/¾ mile: Walk down the road R to the roadside house at Aldhurst Farm (200m).*

ⓓ *Go L over the field to the wood (80m). Follow the path through to the far R corner (200m). In the next field aim across R of centre (150m). Continue into the next field (60m)*

then cross into the adjacent field R. Go L to the end (150m) then R. ➜⑭

⑩ Walk down the road L (300m).

⑪ Opposite the house turn R on the path through trees to the fields. Carry on at R edges to the L wood and into the large field (350m). Go down the L edge as far as the side path in the wood (100m). ☆

⑫ The way is R, obliquely across the field to a bend in the edge of the wood (250m) then L into the corner (50m) but walkers also go round the edge (450m). At the corner go over the ditch to the next field (20m) and straight up the R edge to the top of the ridge (250m).

⑬ At the cross path turn R along the ridge between fields (200m). Turn L & R (20m) to continue in the same direction through the thicket with more bends (350m).

⑭ Continue along the L edge of the fields (200m), L of the stable to the next field (40m) and obliquely L to the road (80m). Opposite, slightly R (25m) pass between gardens to the recreation ground (50m). Cross ½L to the car park (200m).

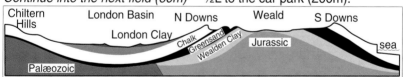

Chiltern Hills — London Basin — London Clay — N Downs — Chalk — Greensand — Wealden Clay — Weald — Jurassic — S Downs — sea — Palæozoic

The **Wealden Clay** is not a soil but a layer more than 1000' thick most of which is unlithified (unsolidified). It formed 125m years ago before the Greensand and Chalk but is exposed in the middle of the Weald. Parts of the layer are not clay but hard rocks such as Horsham Sandstone used for roofing slabs and various Sussex marbles used for memorials. Where the substratum is the clay, the soil is a clay soil. Tiny particles grip water so it is easily water-logged, denying air to roots. Cereals are grown where slopes aid drainage but elsewhere it has wood or pasture. The streams cut little ravines called *gills*. The gills, clay and forest made cultivation and travel difficult so the Weald was thinly populated until hard roads arrived. Oaks were taken for ship building and there was much coppicing to make charcoal for iron working. Siderite nodules out of the clay made this the main iron producing area in Roman times and the Middle Ages. In more recent centuries the clay has been used for brick-making which still continues.

34 Westcott and Denbies Hillside

About 9km/5½ miles with an extension of 1½ km/1 mile; chalk grassland, woods and farmland; splendid views from the North Downs Way; boggy and slippery bits in winter. OS maps 1:25000 146 Dorking, 1:50000 187 Dorking.

Start at Westcott, from the parking area below the church, TQ 140 485, or from the kerbside beside the green nearby; alternatively start at Denbies Hillside car park (NT/pay), TQ 142 153.

The Crown ☎ 01306 885414
The Prince of Wales ☎ 01306 889699

Linking walks 8✳ 12✧
14✳ 22✪ 23★ 35★ 36✳

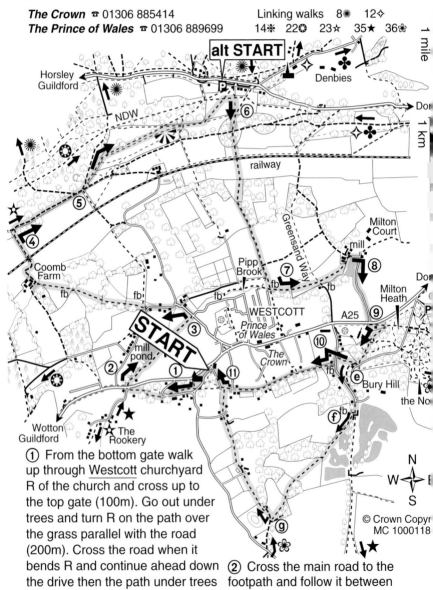

① From the bottom gate walk up through <u>Westcott</u> churchyard R of the church and cross up to the top gate (100m). Go out under trees and turn R on the path over the grass parallel with the road (200m). Cross the road when it bends R and continue ahead down the drive then the path under trees to the road junction (300m). ★✪

② Cross the main road to the footpath and follow it between gardens to the next road (700m).

© Crown Copyr
MC 1000118

68

③ Walk L along the road, over the bridge (150m), round bends L & R, and ahead (200m). On the next L bend enter the R field. Stay ahead along the middle of the narrow field (150m) then the L edge (150m), across the next field to the furthest corner (200m), over the ditch in the next, on over a rise to the far R corner (200m) and through the trees to Coomb Farm (50m). Go R up the track, round the farm, round R & L bends, under the railway (200m) to the wood (200m).

④ Follow the track R outside the fields to the cross path up from the railway into the wood (550m). ✳

⑤ Turn L (40m) then fork R up the edge of the wood (200m). Stay on this path out to grassland and obliquely up the slope to the end of the wood above L (800m). Bear L over the brow of the hill to the cross path (NDW) (200m), then R to the hedge bend (80m). ✧✤ (Denbies Hillside car park 50m L)

⑥ Take the path directly away from the road over the brow of the hill into the wood (150m), straight down, over the level track (100m) to the bottom (300m). Cross the railway and the next field to the corner of the L wood (150m). Go on up the next field near the wood (150m). Out of the field, bear L beside the wood (100m) and stay ahead down the edge of the fields to the Pipp Brook footbridge near the houses of Westcott (500m).

⑦ Don't cross but turn L on the path in the trees and continue along the meadows L of the stream past a footbridge R (350m) to the barnyard (200m) and along the R edge to the exit gate (80m).

⑧ Turn R past the mill and pond to the gates of Milton Court (100m). Follow the drive R but first step in briefly to see the house (450m).

⑨ Cross the main road and take the path L diverging from it into Milton Heath (80m). ✿ At the end of the garden take the side path R and stay ahead under trees up to the drive of Bury Hill (300m). Turn R towards the house (20m) and R beside the garden.

ⓔ *Extension of 1½ km/1 mile: Go L round the garden and down the track to the road (200m). Walk to the end of the road (120m) then along the path in the trees below the Bury Hill fishpond (100m). ★*

ⓕ *Cross the footbridge R and continue on the path between hedges into the corner of a field (350m). Leave the corner on the bisecting line, crossing to the R corner of the L wood (250m). Go up beside the fields to the track across the top (300m).*

ⓖ *Turn R along the track round the hill. Stay ahead on paths and track beside fields, over a farm drive (400m), over a residential road (400m) and down to the end of the fields at Westcott (200m). Turn L to the road (30m). ➜⑪*

⑩ Stay ahead on the R footpath down beside the field to the road (150m). Turn L to the footbridge (50m) and cross it. Go up the path soon between fields and gardens of Westcott (300m). (The 1st side path R, between gardens, leads down to the pubs and shops.) Stay ahead through the complex of house drives (450m) to the next road (100m).

⑪ Turn R to the church (150m).

35 Milton Heath, Squires Farm and Westcott

About 9km/5½ miles with an extension of ¾km/½ mile. A hilly greensand walk through farmland and woods; bluenbells in season.   OS maps 1:25000 146 Dorking, 1:50000 187 Dorking.

Start from Milton Heath main car park, TQ 154 488 (not next to the road), or from Westcott below the church, TQ 140 485 (or at the green on Sundays).

The Crown ☎ 01306 885414   Linking walks   23✿   27✪   34★   36✪   Do

The Prince of Wales ☎ 01306 889699

The Wotton Hatch ☎ 01306 887694

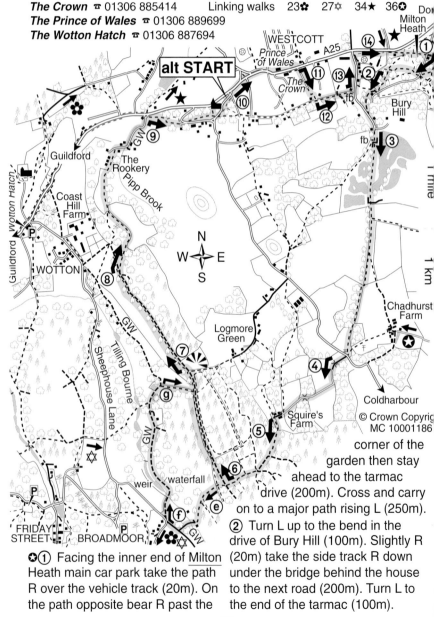

corner of the garden then stay ahead to the tarmac drive (200m). Cross and carry on to a major path rising L (250m).

② Turn L up to the bend in the drive of Bury Hill (100m). Slightly R (20m) take the side track R down under the bridge behind the house to the next road (200m). Turn L to the end of the tarmac (100m).

✪① Facing the inner end of <u>Milton</u> Heath main car park take the path R over the vehicle track (20m). On the path opposite bear R past the

③ Stay ahead on the path under the trees, between ponds (500m) then through fields. Disregard a diverging path L in the 2nd field (350m). Stay at the R edge (150m) then cross to the wood and keep on up the edge (300m). In the next field stay ahead beside trees then across to the top corner (150m).

④ Cross the road and follow the track opposite which becomes a concrete drive. Stay on the drive round several bends and up through Squire's Farm (650m).

⑤ After the garden take the path L into the forest (80m) and up the hillside (200m). At the forest track bear R up to the 5-way junction (150m) and take the steepest path. Stay ahead over the top to the major track, a byway (200m).

ⓔ *Extension of ¾km/½ mile via the* Tillingbourne *valley. Cross the byway and stay ahead over another cross path (60m) to the brow of the hill, down into the valley (300m) then on the drive over the Tilling-bourne and up to the next track (*Greensand Way*) (100m).* ✿✿

ⓕ *Turn R to Broadmoor (100m). At the road bear R on the adjacent track. Stay on this track down over the Tilling (150m), past a waterfall R (100m) and a house R (400m) to the valleyside field R (250m).*

ⓖ *Turn R up the path R beside the wood to the top (200m) then L outside the field.* ➝⑦

⑥ Turn R (200m). Join the parallel path on the L bank and stay on it down to the field with footpath L below (500m).

⑦ Continue briefly beside the field then join the main track R and continue past a side track (120m)

and a field with a view NE. After the view re-join the path L of the track and continue down to the diverging downhill side path R in the trees just after a rising track R (800m).

⑧ Follow the side path R winding down through the trees then beside fields to the lane at The Rookery (900m). Go down the lane R, over the Pipp Brook, round the L bend and on to the main road (350m). ★

⑨ Turn back R on the path up through the trees and join the drive on top (300m). Cross the road and carry on along the path L of the road until opposite the cemetery R (250m). Either cross the road and follow the path down through the trees R of the road or turn L into the churchyard and descend to the main road in Westcott (100m).

⑩ Follow the main road past the shops, the **Prince of Wales** and the **Crown** (400m).

⑪ Soon after the *Crown* (80m) turn R up the side road, School Lane. Keep on to the very top then up the drive and path (250m).

⑫ At the fields turn L along the path behind the gardens and stay ahead down to the road at Milton Street (300m).

⑬ Turn L along the road (250m).

⑭ Just before the main road turn R into the recreation ground and cross the grass to the far L corner (250m). Join the main road with care. Don't cross the road but turn R over the bridge (30m) then diverge R on the path into Milton Heath past a house R to the tarmac drive (400m). Stay ahead past another house R (80m) then turn L into the car park.

36 Nower, North Holmwood and Squire's Farm

About 9½km/6 miles; short cut of 3km/1¾ miles; extension 700m/½ mile; steep start, undulating farmland. OS maps 1:25000 146 Dorking, 1:50000 187 Dorking.

Start from the main car park in Milton Heath, TQ 154 488, or from the kerbside at North Holmwood, parking near the village hall (on Spook Hill), TQ 168 471.

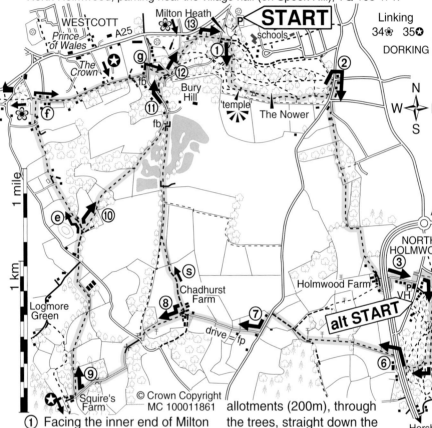

© Crown Copyright MC 100011861

① Facing the inner end of Milton Heath car park take the path R over the vehicle track (20m) and straight up the steep path, avoiding R branches (60m). Stay ahead past the Nower 'temple' on top (300m) to the end of the ridge (500m).

② Turn down L the edge of the park to the gate (100m). Cross the road and follow the pavement R over the rise (100m). Bear L down Ridgeway Road (100m) and take the footpath R just before the bend. Keep on between gardens, across

allotments (200m), through the trees, straight down the next field to the bottom L corner (200m), into the next field (40m), L to the corner (100m) then R between hedges over the rise (200m). At the cross hedge bear L between fields to the farm (150m).

③ At the buildings turn L up over the A24 (50m) or go down under it and up the other side (200m). Go on along the lane into North Holmwood (200m). Just down the road (50m) cross the footbridge R and aim for the church (100m).

72

④ Turn R on the path outside the churchyard up through the trees of Holmwood Common to the clearing (300m). Fork R along the edge and go on through the trees watching out for the first cross path (200m).

⑤ Turn R then stay ahead over several cross paths eventually curving up R to a path near the audible road (200m). Follow this down L to the main road (100m).

⑥ Turn R along the verge (150m). Watch out for a path up steps on the other side, after the last house in the group, and cross the dual carriageway to it (40m). Climb into the field and follow the hedge away from the road (300m). Cross the bridge at the bottom and go straight on aiming for the R edge of the wood (300m). Over the culvert bear R on the track to the gate and go up the next field to the road (250m).

⑦ Go L on the road (100m) and R on the drive to Chadhurst Farm. Pass the farmhouse R and pond L to the end at the barn (600m).

Ⓢ *Short cut of 3km km/1¾ miles: Turn R down the farm track (350m). At the field stay ahead converging on the L edge (200m). Continue between fields then fishing lakes to the first house (800m).* ➚⑪

⑧ Turn R to the end of the barn then take the path in the field round the barn to the top corner (50m) and turn R straight up the field to the corner of the wood R (150m). Bear L along the edge to the next field (100m) and go straight up to the L corner (40m). Cross the road and follow the Squires Farm drive. The drive curves L (150m) round the wood (150m) then bends R (150m) up to the farm (450m). ✪

⑨ Enter the field R just before the buildings and follow the L edge (300m). At the 3rd field cross to the far R corner (250m). Cross the culvert and follow the trees round L. Keep on beside the R hedge until it bends R (200m) then make for the far R corner (100m). Cross the road and follow the track on the other side to the L bend (200m).

ⓔ *Extension of 700m/½ mile: Carry on round the L bend to the end of the track (100m). Stay ahead R of the hillside fields, over a farm drive (300m) and over a road with houses (400m), ultimately up to a path T-junction (150m).* ❀

ⓕ *Turn R. Stay ahead across a complex of drives, behind gardens then between fields and down to the road (800m).*

ⓖ *Turn L on the road (60m) and R on the path up the edge of the field to the tarmac drive (150m).* ➚⑫

⑩ At the bend take the footpath ahead down the R edge of the field to the end of the wood R (300m). Stay ahead across the field to the end of the hedge at the next wood (250m). Keep on outside the hedge of the angling complex and cross the footbridge (400m). Turn L to the end of the path at a house (100m).

⑪ Carry on along the road to the next house R (50m). Soon after it (50m) bear R up the track through the trees (150m). On top join the tarmac drive at the house.

⑫ Turn L and immediately take the downhill side path L into Milton Heath. Stay ahead to the path junction after the garden L (300m).

⑬ Turn R (150m) and cross the tarmac drive. Just past the garden R, turn L to the car park (100m).

37 Brockham, the River Mole and Box Hill

About 9 km5½ miles with an extension of 700mkm/½ mile. Steep slopes; grand views. OS maps 1:25000 146 Dorking, 1:50000 187 Dorking.

Start from Brockham at the rugby car park, TQ 199 499. During rugby events start at the kerbside on the village green, TQ 197 495. The car parks on top of Box Hill (NT/pay), TQ 178 512, are close to the route.

The Inn on the Green ☎ 01737 845101   **The Royal Oak** ☎ 01737 843241
The Watermill ☎ 01306 883248   **The Smith & Western** ☎ 01737 841666

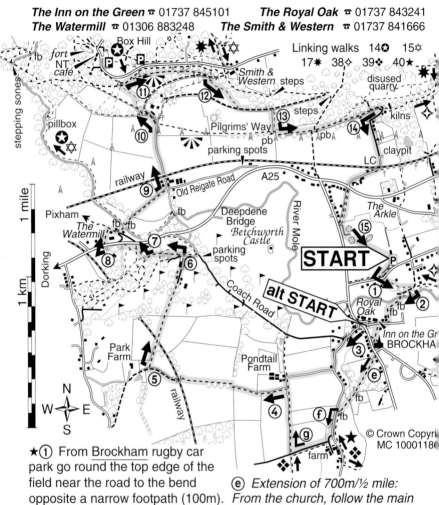

★① From Brockham rugby car park go round the top edge of the field near the road to the bend opposite a narrow footpath (100m). Cross and go up that path (200m).
② At the end take the downhill track back R (200m). Cross the River Mole and stay ahead on the winding path up to the road (200m). Turn R to the village green near the **Inn on the Green** (60m). ❖

ⓔ *Extension of 700m/½ mile: From the church, follow the main road away from the green (50m). Just after Wheelers Lane cross to the footpath R. Follow it over the field diagonally (300m). Keep on obliquely across narrow fields (200m).* ❖ *At the hedge exit to the lane over a footbridge.*

ⓕ *Turn L up the lane (150m) and R on the broad track which curves towards the farm (50m). Take the 1st side track R over the stream. Watch out for side paths at the end of the fields L & R (250m).*

ⓖ *Turn R. Keep to the L edge of the fields to the end of the L field before the farm (400m). Turn L ➔ ④*

③ From the **Royal Oak** cross the main road. Go up Old School Lane and down over the bridge (150m). Stay on the winding road up to the field (200m) then turn R along the drive to Pondtail Farm (350m). At the farm entrance turn L along the edge of the field (50m) then R.

④ Cross the footbridge into the side field. Follow R hedges to the end of the 2nd field (400m) then exit to the adjacent field R (10m). Continue in the same direction, under the railway (400m) and up the curving track until just past the hedge bend 50m R (250m).

⑤ Cross on the path to the hedge bend (50m) and descend R of the hedge (150m). Stay on the same line over the railway, the L corner of the field (150m) and the golf course into the trees (100m). Go on past huts then R of the club house to the R bend at the car park (300m).

⑥ Step into the trees ahead (5m) and go L up the footpath (350m).

⑦ At a L curve, a side path drops R into a bowl-like clearing. Follow it down and join the road (100m). Walk L up the pavement until just past the **Watermill** Inn (200m).

⑧ Cross the road to go down the path L of the pub car park (100m). At the bottom turn R (50m) then L over Castle Mill leat (20m) and R over the River Mole (50m). ❂✿

Keep on over the narrow field and up the next field to the road (400m).

⑨ Walk up the road L (450m).

⑩ When it becomes a drive, fork L up the track (100m). Fork L again under trees to the hillside fields. Disregard a level side path L along the first hedge and follow the rising hedge (100m). At the grass bear R straight up Box Hill. Aim for the trig point on the brow (200m).

⑪ Turn R along the brow of the hill (80m). Don't turn up L at the trees but go on through the top of the next field (300m) then into the trees above (L of) a sunken track. Join this track at a convergence (100m) and go up it briefly (30m) ✳ (**Smith & Western** 150m ahead) then turn R up the bank into the field.

⑫ Descend (50m). Cross the oblique path which ascends L and take the oblique path descending L (300m). Join the track at the bottom and go into the trees. After the field below watch out for the fence and steep side path down R (250m).

⑬ Drop through the trees (200m) and turn L at the foot of the wood. Stay on this path over a downhill track (250m) and join the track from Brockham chalk quarry (450m) down to disused kilns (100m).✧

⑭ Turn R though the gateway near the house. Carry on down the track (100m), round a L bend past more houses then on tarmac over the level crossing (300m) and down to the main road, A25 (300m). Cross to the footpath opposite and follow the edge of the field to the rugby playing field (250m).

⑮ Cross the pitches or go round the L edge to the pavilion and the car park beyond it (400m).

38 Brockham, Pilgrims' Way and Betchworth

About 9 km/5½ miles. Undulating farmland and woods at the foot of the North Downs. OS maps 1:25000 146 Dorking, 1:50000 187 Dorking.

Start from the roadside at Brockham village green, TQ 197 495, or in Church Steet at Betchworth, TQ 210 497 or outside Betchworth Golf Club, TQ 185 500.

Linking 14✲ 15❀ 17★ 18☆ 37✧ 39✪ 40✾

The Dolphin ☎ 01737 842288
The Royal Oak ☎ 01737 843241
Inn on the Green ☎ 01737 845101

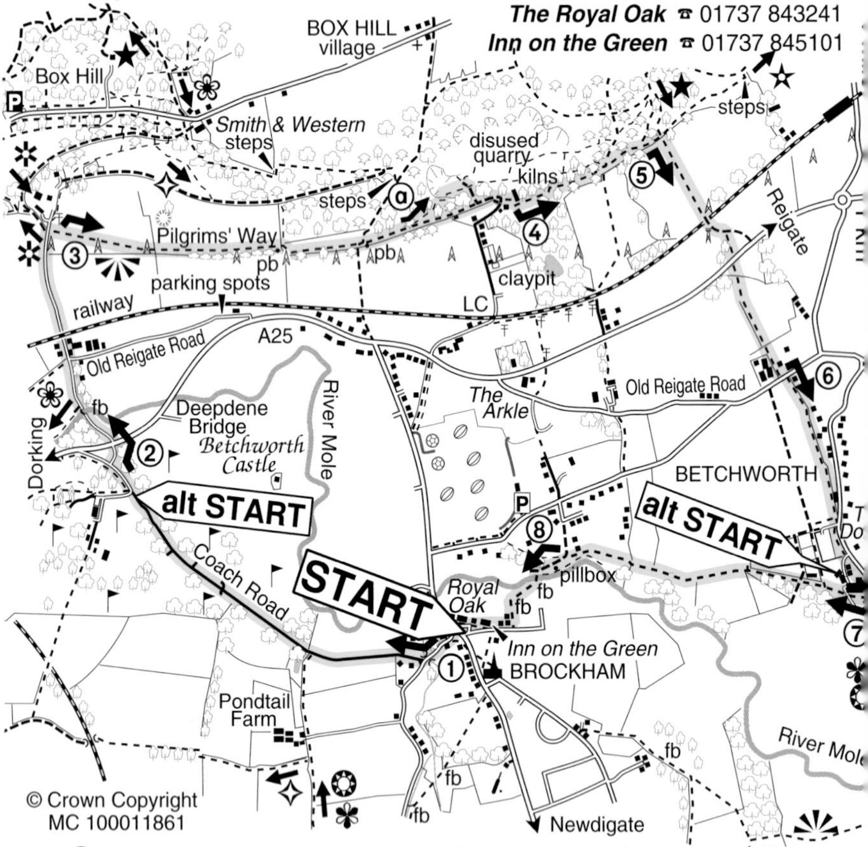

BOX HILL village
Box Hill
P
Smith & Western steps
disused quarry
kilns
steps
steps
Pilgrims' Way
pb
parking spots
pb
claypit
Reigate
railway
LC
Old Reigate Road
A25
Old Reigate Road
The Arkle
River Mole
Deepdene Bridge
Betchworth Castle
fb
Dorking
BETCHWORTH
alt START
alt START
Coach Road
START
Royal Oak
fb
fb
pillbox
Inn on the Green
BROCKHAM
Pondtail Farm
fb
fb
fb
River Mole
Newdigate
© Crown Copyright
MC 100011861

✧① From Brockham village green, at the corner furthest from the church, go up Old School Lane over the rise and down to the brook (150m). After the bridge bear R on the track (old coach road). Stay on this track between fields and golf course all the way to the tarmac drive from the clubhouse (1250m). ② Go down the drive (150m) and branch R to the main road (80m). Cross and go down the lane, past the garden centre and over the River Mole (200m). ❀ Stay ahead to Boxhill Road (150m) and up under the railway (100m) to the diverging track L (400m). ✲★

③ Enter the field R opposite the track. Go straight along the fields (Pilgrim's Way) into the wood at the bottom corner (600m). Go on down round the corner and outside fields past a staggered cross track where the pillbox is level with a pylon R

(300m). Soon after the next pylon watch out for the oblique path up L into the trees (200m). Either stay ahead to the block of lime kilns of Brockham Chalk Quarry (350m) or

(a) *Take the side path rising along the slope into a white cleft then beside the chalk quarry and down into it. Carry on to the exit track R (250m) and follow that down round a L bend to the lime kilns (150m).*

④ Go round the R end of the lime kilns (50m) and on under trees then beside fields past the staggered cross path (300m) and a side path up L (150m). ☆ At the next cross path (70m) turn R into the field.

⑤ Go straight down the field, over the railway (350m) and along the track curving L (50m) then turn R along, L of, the line of trees to the stile (100m). Slightly R cross the road into the opposite field. Follow the path across the fields then between buildings to the road in Betchworth (400m).

⑥ Slightly L (30m) cross to the field opposite and take the path along the L edge (500m). After the field continue on the path R of the pavement then along the road to the **Dolphin** (300m). ❀

⑦ Just after the pub turn R into the churchyard (GW). Follow the path L of the church and out over a drive (100m). Stay ahead beside the wood (350m) then between fields to the vehicle track crossing near houses at Brockham (650m).

⑧ Go down the track L (80m). At the pillbox drop L to the River Mole and carry on along the bank to the footbridge (50m). Cross and follow the path up to the road (200m). Turn R to the village green (100m) and go along the R edge past the **Inn on the Green** and **Royal Oak** to the main road (100m).

Betchworth in the Domesday Book

OS facsimile 1860

This BECESWORDE had a church (eccla) and became East Betchworth. Brockham village developed on it. Becesuuorde is shown as a property of Thorncroft and became West Betchworth or the Castle Estate. These were manors, not houses or villages, but probably had a village. The data was compiled in 1086 but the folios were not made into a book for some years. Officially it was the *Book of Winchester* but the satirical *Domesday* name was in use from the 13th century. It is on display at the National Archives.

LAND OF RICHARD SON OF COUNT GILBERT
Richard himself holds in demesne <u>BECESWORDE</u>   In <u>WOTTON</u> Hundred
Cola held it from king Edward. Then is defended itself for vi hides; now for ii hides. Land for vii ploughs. In demesne is one plough; vi villeins & x bordars with iii ploughs. There are vi serfs; a mill @ x shillings; 3 acres meadow. Woodland @ four xx pigs. From grazing vi pigs. There is a church. TRE & later £ix. Now £viii. (TRE = Time of *Rex* Edward)

39 Stonebridge, Strood Green & Highridge Wood

About 9 km/5½ miles. The extension into Brockham of 1½ km/1 mile and short cut of 800m/½ mile may be combined. Gently undulating farmland; lots of stiles. OS maps 1:25000 146 Dorking, 1:50000 187 Dorking.

Start from the layby opposite the Stonebridge *Royal Oak* TQ 177 479, or, on the extension, from the kerbside near the Brockham *Royal Oak*, TQ 197 495. The car park at Highridge Wood is near the route, TQ 199 470.

Linking 37❖ 38◉ 40✷ 41❄

Royal Oak at Stonebridge
☎ 01306 885420
Royal Oak at Brockham
☎ 01737 843241
Inn on the Green
☎ 01737 845101

© Crown Copyright
MC 100011861   Newdiga

① Just S of the ***Royal Oak*** layby at Stonebridge enter the field. Follow the L edge down and round the corner to the footbridge (400m). Cross. Continue at the L edge and out to the farm drive (550m).

② Pass under the railway (30m). Soon after it enter the field L. Turn R along the hedge to the next field

(40m) then cross diagonally to the furthest corner (300m). Follow the track towards the farm but stay with the L hedge when it diverges (80m). Continue along the L hedge through the fields to the vehicle track between hedges (600m). ❖◉

③ Go R on the track (300m), R into Felton's Farm (40m), L beside the first barn, over the road and into the field opposite (50m).

78

(e) *Extension of 1½ km/1 mile into Brockham: Turn L along the edge past the next exit L (300m), then diverge across the fields to the tree-lined large field (150m). Keep on diagonally and out to the roads (300m) Cross L to the village green (100m). ✳ (The **Royal Oak** and **Inn** are at the far end 150m.)*

(f) *Go round, L of, the churchyard and back out to Wheelers Lane (100m). Carry on along it past the 2nd end of Dodds Park R (300m).*

(g) *Bear L at the next gap between the houses. When the path bends R (450m), cross the field ahead to the top corner (300m). Bear R up past the end of the wood (100m) and R of the next trees (80m).*

(h) *Turn R down the field past a hedge end R and hedge bend L to the corner 70m L of the dense line of trees (300m). Go out to the road (50m) and turn L (100m).* →(5)

(4) Turn R. Keep to the R hedge round the fields to the footbridge R (500m). Cross and go on outside gardens (200m). Over the road, slightly L, continue in the same direction across fields to the next road (300m). Turn R (200m).

(5) At the road junction cross to the L corner of the field (30m). Follow the L edge through the fields to the corner after the L wood (600m). ✳

(6) Don't go into the next field but round the corner under trees and along L edges to the road (500m). Turn R along the road to Strood Green (150m) and L along Tweed Lane to the end field (200m).

(7) After the farm drive R (30m), go L on path outside the field (450m). Continue into Highridge Wood to the broad cross path (100m).

(8) Go R (350m). At the end of the L curve on top watch out for a side path R. Follow it along the edge of the wood to a stile R (200m). Go R, straight across the field (150m).

(s) *Short cut of 800m/½ mile: Walk up the road R over the rise (100m). At the next drive R enter the field L and go straight up to the trees (100m). Turn R along the edge of the wood (200m). Just before the end of the wood turn into the trees and cross to the far edge (200m). In the field cross to the railway bridge (100m) and go under it to the farm drive (100m).*

(t) *Turn R along the drive (150m) and L into the first field. Keep to the edge to the end (400m). Cross the bridge and narrow field (50m).* →(12)

(9) Walk down the road L past the drive of Root Hill Farm L (300m) and on to the side track R at the next house R (100m).

(10) Go along the track, into the field at the end (200m), up round the R edge and over the railway bridge (150m). Walk down the field R to the corner (250m) and across the end to the trees (100m).

(11) In the next field don't follow the R hedge but cross obliquely to the gateway (200m). Cross the foot-bridge to the next field and go up the R edge to the top field (250m). Stay ahead over the middle (towards the centre knoll of the tree covered ridge on the skyline) and down to the gate (400m). Outside converge on the L edge to the L gate (100m).

(12) Go up the farm track between hedges to the road at the edge of Dorking (250m). Follow the road R to the *Royal Oak* layby (300m).

40 Brockham, Betchworth and Gadbrook

About 7 km/4¼ miles with a short cut of 2 km/1¼ miles and two extensions of 900m/½ mile and 2½ km/1½ miles; tranquil; gently undulating farmland on the Greensand; lots of stiles. OS maps 1:25000 146 Dorking, 1:50000 187 Dorking.

Start at Brockham, parking in a side road in the village green, TQ 197 495, or at Betchworth, parking in Church Street, TQ 210 497. There is a car park near ②.

The Inn on the Green ☎ 01737 845101   **The Royal Oak** ☎ 01737 843241
The Dolphin ☎ 01737 842288

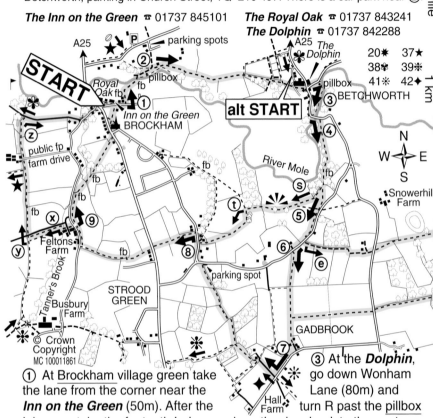

① At Brockham village green take the lane from the corner near the **Inn on the Green** (50m). After the L houses take the footpath L down to the River Mole (200m). Over the river, turn R along the bank (50m) then continue up the track in the trees above the pillbox (100m).

② At the bend take the path along the brow of the hill R of the houses (250m). Stay ahead on this path, between fields above the river (400m), then beside a wood, to Betchworth churchyard (300m). Pass R of the church to the pub (150m) or turn L for Church Street.

③ At the **Dolphin**, go down Wonham Lane (80m) and turn R past the pillbox along the river bank to the next road (300m). Cross the river (60m).

④ After the bridge (30m) enter the field R and follow the path ahead eventually up beside trees (250m), into the wood, down over a bridge (120m), up to the next field (100m) and around the R edge (30m).

Ⓢ *Short cut of 2 km/1¼ miles: Stay ahead beside the wood (80m), along the brow of the hill (400m), through a hedge and on to the end of another small wood R (120m).*

(t) *Turn L past the line of trees (80m) then R down past a hedge end R and hedge bend L into the corner 70m L of the dense line of trees (300m). Go out to the road (50m) and turn L (100m).* ♦(8)

(5) Diverge from the wood to the L hedge (100m). Don't exit just before the wood L but go on along the edge to the next exit after a house (200m). Walk along the road R.

(e) *Extension of 2½ km/1½ miles to Rice Bridge: At the gate (40m) take the track L along the edge of the field (300m), round R & L bends (30m) and past houses to the next road (200m). Cross to the field opposite and aim for the far L corner (150m). Keep on past a hedge bend L (40m) up the lumpy old hedge line (150m), past the belt of trees on top to a line of trees R (100m), then bear R on the path across the field to a protruding corner of field (200m). Bear L along the edge and keep on down to* <u>Rice Bridge</u> *(200m).* ✳

(f) *Don't cross. Turn back up the other path to the corner of the field (30m).*✦ *Disregard paths along the edges and aim out of the corner on the bisecting line. Pass L of a line of trees into the corner at the wood (400m). Keep on through the wood to the next field (120m), along the R edge and over the road (400m). In the field opposite (10m L) go straight on over a ditch (300m) to the raised cross path (300m) then L to the road (200m).* ♦(7)

(6) Just after the next house R (100m) enter the field L and follow the R edge (250m). Continue over the next field to the road (400m).

(7) At Gadbrook go R on the road to the Hall Farm drive L (250m). ✳ Opposite it, turn R along the drive (200m). Fork L of the house. Don't enter the field L but go on along the garden hedge to the field behind (60m). ✳ Keep on through several fields, always near R edges, to the road (600m). Cross slightly L and walk along Wheelers Lane (200m).

(8) Just before the first house L, go L along the edge of the field and straight on to the next road (350m). Cross to the house L (30m). Take the path beside gardens (200m), R over the bridge into the field then L along the hedge to the corner near the road (350m). Go round the corner and on to the gate after the end of the barns opposite (150m).

(x) *Extension of 900m/½ mile: Go over the road, slightly L, into the barnyard, past the barns to the field behind (80m) and on to the far R corner. The RoW is 30m from the R hedge but the path is beside it or the track can be used (250m).*

(y) *Turn R across the track.* ★ *Stay ahead at the L edge, over the farm drive (500m) to the track (300m).* ✤

(z) *Follow the track R to Brockham (550m) and bear L over the bridge up to the village green (100m).*

(9) Stay ahead along the edge (200m). Near the narrow end of the field (at another exit L) the path diverges from the road to a gate (120m). Carry on across the narrow field with a stream (60m) into the corner of a larger field. Cross to the furthest corner diagonally and exit to the road in Brockham (300m). Turn L to the village green (60m). The pubs are at the far end (150m).

41 Dawesgreen, Mynthurst and Strood Green

About 10½ km/6½ miles; gently undulating farmland and woods on the Wealden Clay. OS maps 1:25000 146 Dorking, 1:50000 187 Dorking.

Start from Dawesgreen, parking at the cricket field drive, TQ 217 470.

The Seven Stars ☎ 01306 611254   Linking walks 39✳ 40✳ 42✿ 44☆ 45✪

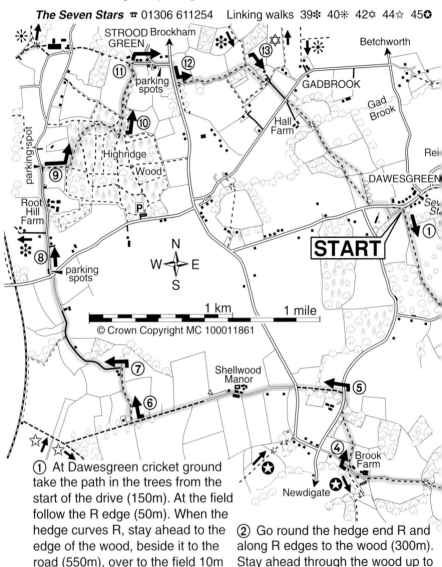

① At Dawesgreen cricket ground take the path in the trees from the start of the drive (150m). At the field follow the R edge (50m). When the hedge curves R, stay ahead to the edge of the wood, beside it to the road (550m), over to the field 10m R, down the L edge (150m), through the thicket between fields, over Hammer Bridge and up to the next field (200m). The path then converges on the R edge (150m).

② Go round the hedge end R and along R edges to the wood (300m). Stay ahead through the wood up to the next field (300m) and up the L edge to the top (100m). Mynthurst Farm is below. Another house is R of it 150m. Aim for the near corner of its garden hedge (250m). ✪

82

③ Just before the hedge, turn R along the farm track until level with the house (50m) then bear ½R up the fields. The hilltop slopes down L. Halfway down is a clump of trees. Aim for this clump (250m) Pass L of it into the top of a field. Diverge from the trees down over the brow to a stile 80m from the top edge (150m). Go through the valley trees, over the stream, to the next field (60m) and up the R edge to Brook Farm (400m). Bear R on the drive past the large buildings R and the house L (50m). Keep on (80m).

④ After the R field take the foot-path R which crosses into the next

The Plough

field (20m). Follow the

GH

R hedge up to the top field (150m) and cross diagonally L down to the corner at the wood (150m). Go on through the trees (60m) then follow the road R past the farm drive L and round the L curve (150m).

Hammer Bridge

② ⑤ Turn L on the track between fields to the next road (300m). Go up the drive opposite past Shellwood Manor R on top (400m). Continue between barns then on the track between fields (750m).✿ Watch out for a house behind the trees R.

⑥ Before the house, take the footpath R at

Mynthurst Farm

the end of the large field. Follow the L hedge to the corner (300m) and up the next field past a house (80m).

⑦ Just after the house join the drive L and stay on it winding and undulating between fields and past several houses to the road (900m).

⑧ Cross and carry on along the lane opposite. ❋ Pass the drive of Root Hill Farm R (450m) and more houses R (100m) (North Downs visible ahead) to a footpath R halfway up the next field (100m) .

⑨ Go straight across the field (150m) into Highridge Wood (20m). Turn L on the cross path along the edge of the wood and round R to a wider path (200m). Turn L on the wider path which curves R into a dip past minor side paths and up to the broad cross path (300m).

⑩ Go L down this broad path soon beside a field (100m). Carry on to the end at Strood Green (350m).❋

⑪ Follow the road R and cross the main road, Middle Street (250m).

⑫ Turn R along the path beside the road then L into the end of the field (120m). Go along the R edge of the fields past a clump of trees R (100m), a side path R (150m) and another clump of trees R (200m).✳

⑬ At the corner turn R into the adjacent field. Go along the L edge (100m), ahead round the garden to the drive (50m) ✿ and out R to the road at Gadbrook (150m). Cross to the drive of Hall Farm but take the footpath diverging L of it to pass outside the garden hedge. Stay ahead at the edge of the field (250m), over the Gad Brook in the trees and on to the field before the wood (200m). The RoW crosses obliquely to the line of trees L of the wood (250m) then follows the line of trees to the road (200m) but the path crosses to the L corner of the wood, into the next field and obliquely L (450m). Turn L along the road (100m) and R across the end of the cricket field (50m).

42 Dawesgreen, the River Mole and Leigh

About 8km/5 miles with an extension of 1½km/1 mile (avoid when roads are busy) and a short cut of 300m/¼ mile; slightly undulating farmland on the Weald Clay, lots of stiles. OS maps 1:25000 146 Dorking, 1:50000 187 Dorking.

Start from Dawesgreen cricket field, TQ 197 495, or from Leigh village green, parking in Church Road, TQ 233 469.

The Seven Stars ☎ 01306 611254
The Plough ☎ 01306 611348

Linking walks
20✷ 40✦
41✿ 43❊

© Crown Copyright MC 100011861

① From Dawesgreen cricket pavilion join the main road via the R corner of the field (60m). Cross and turn L to the stile R (100m). In the field walk away from the road along the line of trees (200m). Cross the next field obliquely to the opposite edge 50m before the far L corner (300m) and go along the L edge in the next field (150m). Stay ahead into the trees, over the Gad Brook (40m) and along the L edge

of the field to the road at the drive of Hall Farm (250m). Cross and go along the drive opposite (170m).✦
② Fork R of the house and turn R immediately on the footpath, R of the thicket, soon passing round a garden to the field (150m). Go L along the edge to the end (350m).
③ Go round the corner R and on to the footbridge (150m). Cross into the adjacent field and follow the L ditch to the road (250m).

④ Turn R on the road to the gate R (100m) and take the track along the L edge of the field (300m), past R & L bends (40m) and houses to the next road (200m). Cross to the field opposite and aim for the far L corner (150m). Go on past the hedge bend L (40m), up the lumpy old hedge line (150m), past the belt of trees R on top to a line of trees R (100m), then bear R over the field on the path to a protruding corner of field (200m). Bear L along the edge and keep on down to the River Mole & Rice Bridge (200m).✳

⑤ Turn round and ascend to the corner of the field (30m). Go along the L edge (30m). When the line of trees curves away L, stay ahead to the far edge about 100m from the L corner (200m). Go on through the trees, across the Gad Brook and over the field parallel with the R hedge (300m). Cross the next, narrow field L obliquely, converging on the R hedge (150m).

Ⓢ *Short cut of 300m/¼ mile:*
Turn into the adjacent field R at the gate and follow the R hedge. Stay ahead to the road (600m), over it and across the first field (100m).

Ⓣ *Over the stream turn R to the next field (50m). Cross diagonally to the corner (400m). Join the road to Leigh village green (100m).* ➔⑨

⑥ Follow the R edge of the field and stay ahead to the road (600m).

Ⓔ *Extension of 1½km/1 mile if traffic is light: Go L along the road to the stile R just after the house L on the bend (250m). In the field make for the footbridge slightly R (200m) and go on near the L edge over another stream (100m) to the narrow end of the field (150m).*

Ⓕ *Join the drive of Burys Court School and turn L. Stay ahead to the L bend outside the corner of the first large field R (750m).* ✲

Ⓖ *Just after the corner turn R into the trees and carry on along the horse track between fields and past a wood L (450m). At the end of the next field ignore a side path L (200m) and carry on. Watch out for a side path R just before the end of the adjacent field (150m).*

Ⓗ *Cross the hedge and turn L beside it (30m). Go round the corner R and on at the edge to the next corner at trees (300m).* ➔⑧

⑦ Cross to the field opposite. Follow the L edge initially then make for the bottom R corner (200m). Cross the footbridge then stay ahead over the fences (150m) and along the edge of the field (100m). When the trees curve R, cross the field to the protruding hedge corner (200m) and go on at the R edge of the next field (200m). In the next field fork R across to the far R corner (300m).

⑧ Cross the hedge and turn R through the trees over the bridge (30m). Cross the field to the far R corner (150m) and keep on past Leigh church to the green near the **Plough** (200m).

⑨ From Leigh village green walk along Clayhill Road all the way to the wood R (750m). ✿

⑩ Turn R into the field and follow the edge of the wood (350m). At the corner of the wood go straight up the field to the top L corner (250m) and ahead to the next road in Dawesgreen (130m). Turn R on the pavement for the **Seven Stars** (150m) or L for the cricket field.

43 Leigh to Irons Bottom

About 10 km/6 miles with a short cut of 3½ km/2 miles; gently undulating farmland, arable and pasture, on the Weald Clay; lots of stiles.
OS maps 1:25000 146 Dorking, 1:50000 187 Dorking.

Start from Leigh, parking beside Church Road, TQ 224 469, or at Ironsbottom parking at the roadside opposite the *Three Horseshoes*, TQ 249 462.

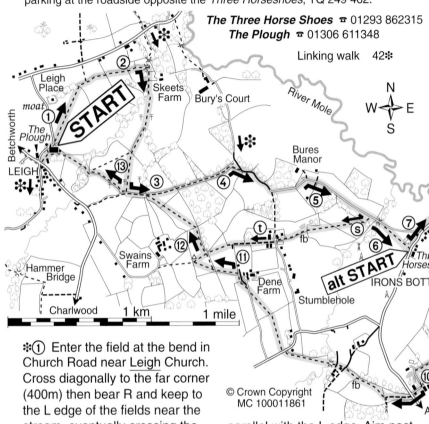

The Three Horse Shoes ☎ 01293 862315
The Plough ☎ 01306 611348

Linking walk 42❉

© Crown Copyright
MC 100011861

❉① Enter the field at the bend in Church Road near Leigh Church. Cross diagonally to the far corner (400m) then bear R and keep to the L edge of the fields near the stream, eventually crossing the bridge at a larger stream (500m)

② Turn R. Cross the fences near Skeets Farm (100m) and carry on at the edge of the field (100m). When the trees (and stream) curve away R, stay ahead over the field to the protruding hedge-corner at the end of a clump of trees (200m). Go on along the R edge of the next field (200m). In the next field the path forks. Fork L across the field towards the distant rising fields and parallel with the L edge. Aim past the R electricity pole to the stile in the end hedge (300m).

③ Cross the stile and turn L. Stay at the L hedge through the fields (400m) and ahead L of the wood (200m). Keep on between fields and eventually fork R under trees to a major track (250m).

④ Follow the winding track R (300m). Disregard the track forking R and carry on round the L bend on the drive past a house R (250m).

86

⑤ Turn R on the larger drive (from Bures Manor) and keep on past the wood R and narrow field R towards the bridge in the trees (550m).

Ⓢ *Short cut of 3½ km/2 miles: (possibly after going to the pub in Irons Bottom). Turn off 50m before the bridge across the narrow field slightly R (60m). Continue ½R over the fields (towards a distant house) (400m) and along the hedge L of the house and garden (200m).*

Ⓣ *Cross the farm drive and stay ahead on the track between barns then fields (350m). Enter the field ahead and make for the top corner (150m). Cross into the next field (with trig point).* ➔⑫

Sidlow
A217

⑥ Stay on the drive (50m). Soon after the bridge (60m) diverge R on the footpath across the field towards the row of houses and join the road opposite the ***Three Horseshoes*** in Irons Bottom (250m).

⑦ Follow the pavement L, round a R bend to the next R bend with houses L (500m).

⑧ Just round this bend, cross to the field opposite and go up the L edge past the belt of trees (450m). In the field above turn R along the hedge (70m) then L up the edge of the wood and on to the top of the field (Reigate visible L) (250m).

⑨ Turn R on the drive past the pond and house L and continue into the field ahead (70m). Follow the L edge of the fields to the wood (250m) then go up L round the corner of the wood by the barn (50m) and on along the R edge of the fields. Stay ahead to the tarmac drive from the house R (400m).

⑩ Turn L round the garden (100m) and go round the R bend to another drive and on between buildings to the road (100m). Cross into the field opposite and bear R down to the gate (200m). In the next field make for the bottom R corner (250m). Go over the bridge into the next field and across to the R corner near the house (100m). Stay ahead over the track, between the garden L and field R, over the farm drive, down over the footbridge (100m) and straight up the field to follow the R edge (avoid gates R) to the road (300m).

⑪ Slightly L (20m) cross into the field opposite and go straight over (towards Dene Farm above) (250m). In the next field bear L to the top L corner (200m). Cross the drive and go up to the top R corner of the field (80m). Keep on next to the farm drive (50m) then turn L in the field and follow the L edge to the next field (180m). Aim out of the corner on the bisecting line up to the trig point (150m) then turn back to the R edge (100m)

⑫ Go down beside the trees (200m) then obliquely L over the fields to the bottom hedge at the L corner (400m). Go on (L) along the track with the hedge R (150m).

⑬ Watch out for a side path R before the end of the adjacent field. Cross into the field and turn L along the hedge. Follow it round corner (30m) and on to the next corner at trees (300m). Cross the hedge and turn R though the trees over the bridge (30m). Cross the field to the far R corner (150m) and keep on past Leigh church to the green near the ***Plough*** (200m).

44 Holmwood Common and Ewood

About 8¾ km/5½ miles with an extension to Beare Green of 1¼ km/¾ mile and a short cut of 800m/½ mile. Gently undulating farmland and the Common on Wealden Clay. OS maps 1:25000 146 Dorking, 1:50000 187 Dorking.

Start at Mill Road car park, South Holmwood, TQ 172 451.

Linking walks
28✦ 41☆ 45◇

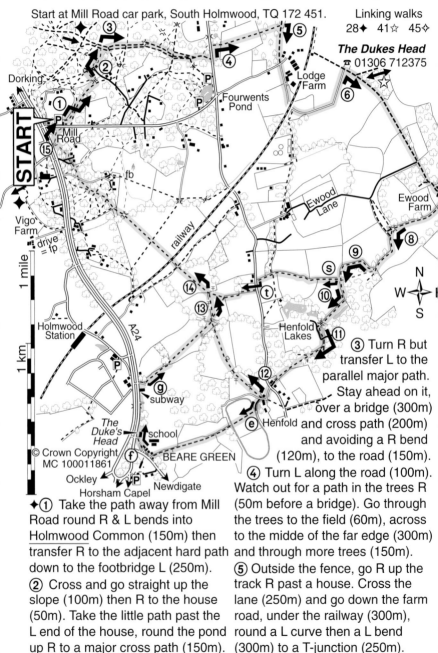

The Dukes Head
☎ 01306 712375

✦① Take the path away from Mill Road round R & L bends into Holmwood Common (150m) then transfer R to the adjacent hard path down to the footbridge L (250m).

② Cross and go straight up the slope (100m) then R to the house (50m). Take the little path past the L end of the house, round the pond up R to a major cross path (150m).

③ Turn R but transfer L to the parallel major path. Stay ahead on it, over a bridge (300m) and cross path (200m) and avoiding a R bend (120m), to the road (150m).

④ Turn L along the road (100m). Watch out for a path in the trees R (50m before a bridge). Go through the trees to the field (60m), across to the midde of the far edge (300m) and through more trees (150m).

⑤ Outside the fence, go R up the track R past a house. Cross the lane (250m) and go down the farm road, under the railway (300m), round a L curve then a L bend (300m) to a T-junction (250m).

⑥ Go R on the track past a branch track L (100m).☆ Keep on beside fields R (600m) then through trees (250m) and down the tarmac drive to Old Ewood Farmhouse (50m). ✧

⑦ Turn R on the bridleway into the field and along the R edge (450m).

⑧ After the bridge turn L and converge on the R hedge (50m). Follow the hedge round a R bend (100m) and on to the wood (200m).

⑨ The public footpath is much obscured so turn R and keep to paths round the edge outside the field. Pass L round a corner (100m) and another (150m) to the side path R in the next field (80m).

ⓢ *Short cut of 800m/½ mile: Follow this path along the R edge of the fields to the road (600m).*

ⓣ *Turn L along the road (80m) and R into the end of the first field. Follow the L edge to the end (80m) then continue in the adjacent field L (100m). Cross the next field to the R corner gateway (100m).* ➜⑭

⑩ Stay ahead outside the field (100m) then cross the bridge into it. Turn L into the enclosure with the long pond (30m) and go along the fence R into the trees (250m).

⑪ After the footbridge, curve L on the path beside the pond then keep to tracks and paths inside the edge of the wood up round R. After the field R stay ahead ever upwards to the top then beside fields to the houses and road (600m). Go up the Henfold drive opposite (100m) and turn R after the first house.

ⓔ *Extension of 1¼ km/¾ mile: After the barn, follow the garden fence round L (100m). Cross the gallop circuit between fences and stay ahead at the R edge (800m).*

ⓕ *At the road in Beare Green, turn R along the verge and keep on past the frontages to the A24 at the **Dukes Head** (150m). Carry on along the pavement to the drive R soon after the subway (300m).*

ⓖ *Turn R beside the drive (50m) and L into the field. Converge on the L hedge and cross it at the trees (200m). Aim along the next field into the R extremity (400m). Cross the L bridge in the trees.* ➜⑬

⑫ Turn into the first large field R (40m). Diverging from the drive, go down the middle and through the trees (300m). In the next field pass L of the clump of trees down to a footbridge hidden in the trees at the bottom, about 100m from the R corner (300m). Cross the footbridge and the corner of the next field and another footbridge (40m).

⑬ Just along the R hedge (15m) cross to the adjacent field and go L to the gateway in the corner (150m).

⑭ Outside the gateway bear L over a slight rise to the L end of the clump of trees (250m). Stay ahead across the narrow field (50m), the railway and the large field through a 4-way path junction (200m) towards the tree lined corner (250m). Cross the stream 50m R of the corner and go on into the trees at the corner of Holmwood Common (80m). Stay ahead past several side paths to a fork (200m) and bear R to the lane (80m). Continue opposite down to the houses (100m) and past the frontages (40m). After the 2nd drive fork L to the war memorial near the A24 at South Holmwood (150m).

⑮ Turn R on the other path away from the A24 across a corner of the Common to the car park (150m).

45 Parkgate, Ewood and Shellwood Cross

About 8½ km/5½ miles with a short cut of 2½ km/1½ miles; farmland and woods on the Wealden Clay. OS maps 1:25000 146 Dorking, 1:50000 187 Dorking.

Start from the layby opposite the *Surrey Oaks* at Parkgate, TQ 205 436.

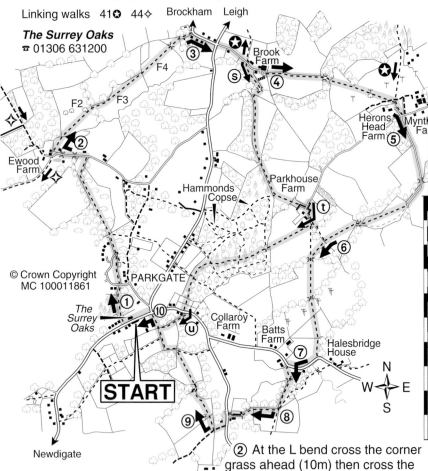

Linking walks 41✪ 44◇

The Surrey Oaks
☎ 01306 631200

© Crown Copyright
MC 100011861

① From the **Surrey Oaks**, take the footpath into the trees between the pub garden and the next house (300m). Stay ahead over a road, down the R edge of the green (200m) then through scrub, then beside a large field L (600m).After the scrub, follow the path into a small field and R along the hedge to the road (150m). Turn L down the road to Ewood Farm (300m).◇

② At the L bend cross the corner grass ahead (10m) then cross the field R to the gate at the corner of the wood (100m). In Field 2, cross ½R to the trees at the far edge, 100m from the R corner (300m) (the RoW is direct but it may be better go round the edge) then stay ahead: F3 near the L edge (Shellwood Manor above L)(400m), F4 across to the footbridge (250m), F5 to the L corner (80mm) F6 to the road (100m). ✪

③ Walk down the road R to the junction, <u>Shellwood</u> Cross (200m). Opposite, carry on along the drive of Brook Farm past the first house to the end of the L field (250m). ✪

Ⓢ *Short cut of 2½ km/1½ miles: Enter the R field. Diverge from the drive into the narrow extremity of the field (200m). After the bridge cross the narrow field to the R corner (50m) and go on through the long field L of the wood to the top corner (450m). Stay ahead past a path from <u>Hammonds Copse</u> R (250m) to <u>Parkhouse Farm</u> (250m).*

Ⓣ *Turn L on the drive (30m) and R into the field. Skirt round the R edge outside the farm almost to the wooded corner (200m) then cross to the adjacent field R behind the farm. Go straight over the middle to the wood, Hammonds Copse. Aim for the R end of the obtruding portion of hedge (350m). Stay on the same path through the wood eventually curving L near fields R to the far edge (700m). Cross paddocks to the road (100m).*

Ⓤ *Cross to the L corner of the garden (20m) and go up the R edge of two fields to a T-junction of paths (200m). Turn R. ➔⑩*

④ Stay on the drive past the next house to the final R bend (150m), ahead through the field R of the fence (400m), into trees and over the stream (30m). In the next field converge on the top L edge to the end of the trees (150m) then aim for the nearest house ahead. Make your way down to the hedge corner L of the house, crossing a track just before it (300m). Follow the hedge round to the estate road from Mynthurst Farm L (100m).

⑤ Cross it and go down the side road opposite, over a bridge at the wood (450m) and round R (200m). At the L bend, enter the long field ahead and make for the far R corner beside the wood (350m). Cross to the next field (30m) and diverge from the L trees to the middle of the far edge (250m).

⑥ Follow the L edge of the next field (150m) then cross to the adjacent field L. Aim slightly R over the rise and down to a footbridge (300m). In subsequent fields diverge from the L edge over the rise towards a house seen through a gap in the trees (250m). Near the corner, cross the fence to the trees and follow the R edge of the gill (little ravine) to the road (150m).

⑦ Turn R up the verge to the 2nd house L (250m). Beside it, take the path between fields down to the stream (100m) and go up the next field to the top R corner (200m).

⑧ Bear R along the edge of the top field (150m). Go on through the trees then beside the garden wall to the road (200m). Follow the road L to the side track R (80m).

⑨ Along the track (100m) turn into the first field R and go down the edge to a stile 20m from the corner (100m). Carry on straight down to the bottom gateway (200m). Cross the valley slightly R to the gateway of the field opposite (60m) and go straight up to the top L corner (350m). In the next field follow the L edge round the corner (80m) and up to the trees (150m).

⑩ Stay ahead between fields to the road (100m). Cross to the pavement and turn L to the *Surrey Oaks* (150m).

The **A24** out of Dorking to Horsham was a new road in 1755 when the turnpike acts ushered in an era of road improvement. The previous way to Horsham was over the top at Coldharbour, in places only wide enough for single file walkers. The carriage route from Horsham to London was via Canterbury!

Abinger was ABINCEBORNE in the Domesday Book. The parish stretches 9 miles southwards from the top of the Downs. Abinger Common is the main village (as well as the common land), the central settlement of the several that make up the parish. The Manor House is 17th century and was built by John Evelyn, the diarist. In its garden is the motte of the Norman house. Enclosed in a shed in the next field is the remains of a mesolithic dwelling excavated by Louis Leakey while on leave from Kenya in 1950, at that time, the oldest house known in Britain. The church, St James, was a 12th and 13th century building wrecked by a flying bomb in 1944 but rebuilt in the original form. Points of interest: post-bomb Norman windows in the nave; two large tie beams in the chancel which are re-used 13th century timbers; list of Rectors from 1283 which also shows the Evelyns have been patrons for the last 350 years; the stocks outside the churchyard. The 1934 Abinger Pageant in aid of the church was put together by E M Forster and Vaughan Williams who lived nearby.

Abinger Bottom is a small hamlet. Greenwich Observatory had an out-station here, 1924-57 - now demolished. It monitored the Earth's magnetic field until electrification of the railways disturbed its environment then became the bomb-proof broadcast station for the Greenwich time-signal during World War II.

Abinger Hammer had a hammer mill. It is one settlement within the large Domesday Book Manor of Abinger, The blacksmith clock replaced an earlier one in 1909. Darwin did his experiments with earthworms on the Roman mosaic floor at Abinger Hall. Abinger Hammer Mill, 1557-1787, was the most northerly Wealden iron works and produced 150 tons of wrought iron p.a. Only one wall of it remains. Blooms and pigs were bought in from bloomeries and blast furnaces elsewhere and heated and hammered to beat out slag and burn off carbon. The mill drove bellows and other machinery as well as a hammer. The mill pond became the first large scale watercress farm in Britain in 1850.

Abinger Mill was demolished early in the 20th century, the millhouse remaining. It was of very ancient building and probably occupied the site of the Domesday Book corn mill assessed @ 6 shillings. When converted for making copper household utensils in 1622 it had been a gunpowder mill. By the end of the century it was a flour mill again and is recorded by the Water Resources Survey in 1851 as producing 40 sacks per week.

Anstiebury is a late iron Age promontory hillfort of 200-100BC. It has a central area of 11 acres within several circular defensive mounds and post holes which suggest a stockade. There is evidence it was dismantled, possibly as a consequence of the arrival of the Romans. The *bury* is presumably derived from *buhr*, Saxon fort. There was a Saxon word *anstig* meaning a path for one ie narrow approach. This area was the Domesday Book manor of HANSTEGA.

Barrows are burial mounds. In this area all are bowl barrows of the Bronze Age (approx 2500 - 700 BC). They usually had ring ditches giving them the profile of an inverted bowl. The early ones had burials; the later ones, urns with cremated remains. Surviving barrows are often in prominent positions, possibly on territorial boundaries. Many will have been lost to the plough and erosion.

Beare Green is a hamlet of Capel. Its name may relate to a Capel landowner called Bere who appears in 14th century court rolls. The area of houses and shops which developed around Holmwood Station is part of Beare Green, cut off from the old part at the green by the enlargement of the A24 in the 1960s.

Betchworth has two entries in the Domesday Book, BECESWORDE, a manor in its own right and BECESUUORDE, appended to the manor of Thorncroft. The name probably derives from a Saxon owner's name *Becci + worþ*, farm. The present village is a scatter of ribbon developments. The parish boundaries are the top of the Downs and the Gadbrook. The church, St Michael, is likely to be on the site of the Domesday Book church but its earliest fabric, the north wall, is Norman, around 1200. The advowson was given to St Mary Overie in 1199 (now Southwark Catherdral) but after the Dissolution went to Windsor.

Bocketts Farm, owned by Surrey County Council, runs as a commercial farm but is open to visitors and keeps rare breeds. The car park is used by walkers but groups need permission to park. The gates are locked at night.

Bookham appeared in a charter of 675 for a grant by Frithwald, sub-king of Surrey, to Chertsey Abbey of 20 dwellings at *Bocham cum Effingham*. In the Domesday Book there were two manors at BOCHEHA . The larger, rated at 13 hides with church and mill, was owned by Chertsey Abbey and became Great Bookham; the smaller, 2 hides, was owned by William of Braose. After the Dissolution of the Monasteries, Great Bookham was granted in 1550 to the Howards of Effingham. *Bocham* probably derived from Saxon *homestead or hamlet near the beeches*. The church of Great Bookham, St Nicholas, probably has stones of the Domesday Book church; the pillar capitals of the south aisle suggest a date of around 1150.

Bookham Common is the commons of Great and Little Bookham which were given to the National Trust in 1920 together with the adjacent Banks Common, 170 ha/370 acres in all. Historically, land that was uneconomical for ploughing was the waste left for communal grazing and timber. London Clay underlies most of the Common but there are patches of residual Ice Age sand and gravel. The ponds were developed for fish farming in the 17th century but the ancient owner, Chertsey Abbey, could well have started them. The Common has been intensely studied by the London Natural History Society since the 1940s.

Box Hill has long been renowned for its beauty, perhaps because of the planned tree-planting and its striking profile and views on the bluff of the North Downs at the Mole gap. Undercutting by the River Mole has given it white cliffs and steep paths. The proximity to London made a popular venue for visitors and day-trippers even before the coming of the railway in Victorian times. The view point is a memorial for Leopold Salomons, 1842-1915, who gave it to the nation in 1914. The National Trust buildings were cottages of Fort workers. John Logie Baird, 1888-1946, the television inventor, lived at the house near the NT shop for a few years around 1930 and gave TV demonstrations there. The Labilliere stone denotes the head-down burial in 1800 of Peter Labillière, latterly a Dorking eccentric, but earlier an Army officer and political agitator. Flint Cottage was the home of George Meredith, 1828-1909, the Victorian novelist and literary figure. The Tower is Broadwood's Folly built around 1820 by Thomas Broadwood, the piano maker, who owned Juniper Hall. The Zig Zag road is much used by endurance cyclists including the 2012 Olympics.

Brockham was part of Domesday Book Betchworth but was detached as a separate manor around 1220 and became a separate parish in 1868. The village has a splendid Victorian church, overlooking the green, built of Reigate Stone and consecrated in 1847. The substantial Borough Bridge over the River Mole was built in 1737, leaving a mystery as to how it was financed.

Brockham Chalk Quarry was owned by the Brockham Brick Company from about 1875. It made bricks from the Gault Clay on the site south of the kilns, mined the Upper Greensand for hearthstone and quarried chalk. The kilns were for roasting the chalk to make quicklime for mortar. The company had a private railway siding and its own narrow gauge system for trucks moved by horse and winch. Brick making ceased in 1910, mining in 1925 and lime production in 1936. The site is now owned by Surrey County Council and conserved for its wildlife and historic significance.

Buckinghill Farm house on Stane Street has medieval and 17th century parts with timbers dated to 1414 and a Horsham slate roof.

Buckland is BOCHELANT in the Domesday Book, a manor with a mill and church. The old parish boundaries which probably correspond to the manor's make it typical of the North Downs stretching from the top of the chalk ridge over the Lower Greensand to the south. The delightful village green is spoiled by the A25. The house, Yewdells, has a small windmill thought to have been built mid 19th century as a sawmill. The church, St Mary the Virgin, with ironstone walls, though much restored in 1860 appears to have been built around 1380; the 14th century timber roof suggests the walls are ancient. The bell turret is supported on oak legs in the nave. The splendid timber spiral staircase to the bell chamber was added in 1860.

The **Burford Bridge Hotel** took this name in 1905 but is on the site of a very ancient inn. Of its many famous visitors Keats is said to have composed Endymion here and Nelson dallied with Emma Hamilton before Trafalgar.

Capel was part of Domesday Book Dorking and is first called *Chapelle* in the Assize records of 1215. It appears to have been *Hewechne* in 1180 probably of the same derivation as *Ewekenes* Farm. A charter of 1130 has the church of Dorking c*um Capella de la Wachna* which would have been a chapel of ease. This chapel seems to have become a parish church around 1300 and is incorporated into the Victorian church of 1860, St John the Baptist. Three lancet windows of 1190 style in the south wall and the piscina may be survivals from the documented early chapel.

Castle Mill on the River Mole ceased milling in 1952 but its machinery has been restored. It probably stands on the site of the Domesday Book mill of Betchworth which by 1760 was the Betchworth Castle estate. The weir raised the level to send water into the very short leat.

Chapel Farm takes its name from the ruin opposite of which nothing certain is known. Merton Abbey owned the manor of Polesden Lacey in the medieval period so the chapel was probably built for the Merton estate.

A **chapel of ease** traditionally is a secondary church established in an existing parish to make it easier for parishioners to worship. Historically they also provided a way of accommodating increased population and many went on to become parish churches as ecclesiastical parishes subdivided.

Cherkley Court is a grand Victorian mansion built in the 1860s and largely rebuilt in 1893 after a fire. From 1910 to 1964 it was the country home of Lord Beaverbrook, newspaper owner and politician, so had numerous famous visitors including Rudyard Kipling, Winston Churchill and H G Wells. It has been maintained by a foundation and open to the public.

Coldharbour is a hamlet of the parish of Capel but acquired its own church, Christ Church, in 1848. It may be the village of the Domesday Book manor HANSTEGE. The Surrey book of place-names devotes two pages to the origin of the present name without drawing firm conclusions. In Britain there are 300 small settlements or houses with the name and it appears to be distributed likewise in Germany as *Kaltenherburg*. It could mean a place of shelter from cold but it is more likely that harbour or haven simply meant dwelling place. The curved concrete structure in front of the pub is the old village water cistern.

Colley Hill would have taken its name from Colley Farm which was *Colelie* in 1180 and probably derives from Anglo Saxon *col leah*, (char)coal clearing.

Denbies Hillside is a short section of the North Downs kept clear of trees with a splendid view and a National Trust car park. It was the site of the house Denbies which was razed in the 1950s.

Denbies Vinyard is the largest in Britain with 265 acres/1.07 km^2 under vines, started in 1986. About 300,000 litres are produced a year. The visitors' centre has 300,000 visitors pa. In the 1850s the estate and grand house were the country seat of Thomas Cubitt the master builder.

Dorking was DORCHINGES in the Domesday Book, a large manor in the Royal demesne. It was used to endow the Earldom of Surrey for William de Warenne. The name may derive from the Anglo-Saxon personal name *Deorc* + ~ingas (people). The estate stretched southwards from the top of the chalk downs over the Lower Greensand to the Wealden Clay. The town sits on the Pipp Brook to the side of the River Mole at the opening to the cleft in the North Downs. It was a market town, stated in 1378 to be from time immemorial. There used to be a Shrove Tuesday football match played across the town by a large and violent crowd up to the early 19th century. The town church, St Martin, was made grand by the rebuilding in 1835-37 and spacious by the use of cast iron pillars but the pilasters in the chancel date to mid 12th century.

Effingham was a Saxon Hundred as well as a manor. King Æthelstan in 933 confirmed the Abbey of Chertsey's ownership of the manor. Its ~*ing* name probably derives from Æffa's people + home. The village is in the line of early settlements along the foot of the North Downs where streams spring from the chalk over the edge of the London Clay. William Howard was granted the manor in 1550 by Queen Mary and became a baron in 1554. The name is most widely known because the Lord High Admiral at the time of the Armada was Charles, second Lord Howard of Effingham; his flagship was the first Ark Royal which is used as the village logo. This Howard was also a diplomat and patron of the actors who became the Admirals' Men of the Shakespearian period. Effingham Church, St Lawrence, has been much rebuilt and the oldest fabric is a 13th century window remnant in the south transept. Merton Abbey held the advowsen but annexed the rectory estate, with the pope's permission, and endowed a vicarage. Barnes Wallace is buried in the churchyard.

Effingham Common is a level grassland with clumps of trees, probably left from time immemorial because the London Clay makes it unworthy of cultivation. To prevent development it was registered as Common Land in 1976 and four properties have commoners' rights of grazing and estovers.

Effingham Junction is the name of the residential area and station as well as the meeting of rails. The chief line (Guildford New Line) was part of L&SWR's infill of suburban lines. The branch through Bookham Common was built at the same time in 1885 to link it to Leatherhead and the London-Horsham Line. The large sheds are a depot for special trains used to clear the tracks of ice, etc.

John **Evelyn** the Diarist, 1620-1706, was the best known member of the family who still live at Wotton. His diary, covering eight decades, published in 1818 is a rich source for historians because of his interests, experience, friends in high places and the period: the Civil War to Queen Anne, the Thames freezing over, re-building of St Paul's, etc, etc. He was a friend of Robert Boyle, Pepys and Christopher Wren. During th Civil War he spent some years in France, Italy and Holland turning himself into an authority on gardens and architecture. His letter to Robert Boyle suggesting a College for Science in London is credited with the inception of the Royal Society of which he was a founder member.

Ewhurst is first heard of in 1179 as *Iuherst*, presumed to derive from yew wood. It was part of Domesday Book Gomshall but became a separate royal estate when Henry II hived off the northern portion in the 12th century. The parish is 6 miles long from Pitch Hill to the Sussex border but only 2 miles wide. The church, SS Peter & Paul, was founded by Merton Priory as a chapel-of-ease to Shere around 1140 so there must have been a village in early times. Largely rebuilt in 1838 (Gothic Revival), it has a Norman font, doorway and window.

Ewood or Iwood was an early hunting area belonging to Dorking Manor of the Earls of Surrey, and contrasted in documents with Holmwood. By 1312 it had the status of a small medieval manor. Ewood Old Farmhouse is Grade II listed, late 16th century. A corn mill at Ewood Farm was preceded by an iron works with a large pond, now filled in. Its dam was 190m long and nearly 3m deep. The lease of 1554 indicates it worked in conjunction with a hammer mill in Leigh (near Hammer footbridge) of which only cinders and documents remain.

Forest Green first appears in a document of around 1598 where it is also called Folles Green. The land has been part of the Evelyn Estates attached to Wotton but was most likely part of Domesday Book Ockley. It lies just off the Greensand on the Wealden Clay . The Oke Brook runs through the village on its way from Holmesbury and Leith Hills to the Arun and English Channel and formerly had a mill. The church, Holy Trinity, is Victorian.

The **forts** at Denbies and Box Hill are misnamed. They were mobilisation depots in the chain of defences from Guildford to Epping built in the 1890s to guard against invasion while the army and navy were scattered across the Empire. They had store rooms and offices below ground level, enclosed by an earth mound and gun emplacements nearby. France was perceived the likely aggressor but the panic had started in 1871 with *The Battle of Dorking*, an anonymous story in *Blackwood's Edinburgh Magazine*, about a German army continuing to Britain after the Franco-Prussian War. This was the origin of the genre of "What if" war stories.   *The Battle of Dorking* G T Chesney 1997 OUP 44pp

Friday Street is a hamlet in the valley of a tributary of the Tilling on the lower slopes of Leith Hill. The origin of the name is obscure; there are several other places with the name and the only common factor appears to be that they are small remote settlements. The large pond is probably the mill pond for the Domesday Book mill of Wotton. In 1579 it was a corn mill but closed in 1736. The stream appears to be nameless but lower down is dammed into numerous fish ponds like the Tillingbourne. The pub is named the *Stephan Langton* because of the tale the great man was born here. The origin of this myth is Martin Tupper's Victorian novel *Stephen Langton*; his birthplace is unknown.

Stephan Langton is first heard of teaching in Paris around 1200 and became the foremost scholar and theologian of his day. He came to the attention of the Pope, moved to Rome and became a cardinal in 1206. The monks of Canterbury elected him Archbishop and he was consecrated in 1207 to the fury of King John who wanted John de Grey. The monks were ejected and he was kept out of England for six years. Innocent III threatened to depose King John in favour of Phillip of France if the Archbishop was not allowed in to his See so he eventually came to England. Stephan Langton was conciliatory in all his dealings and in later years held out against the Pope on behalf of the English church. He initiated the present Canon Law at the Council of Odney in 1215. He mediated between King John and the Barons and may have been the final drafter of Magna Carta which was more universal than the earlier compilations of baronial demands. He died in 1228 at Slindon near Arundel.

The **Gadbrook** drains to the River Mole. Presumably it gets its name from the farm (*gat* and *gad* names usually derive from goat) and gave it to the hamlet.

Great Ridings Wood, managed by the Woodland Trust, forms a fifth of this 150 ha area of woodland mostly in private ownership. The main north-south track is called Old London Road which was probably a drove road for taking sheep to graze on the North Downs and a packhorse route from the industrial Tilling valley. The mound along the west side of the track is the ancient marker of the Woking and Copthorne Hundreds. West of this boundary the area of large forest oaks is fairly ancient but the rest is plantation or fields colonised by ash trees more recently. Woodland predominates here because the wet area of London Clay makes the land unsuitable for farming. The contiguous wood to the north has the moat of the medieval Great Lee manor house.

The **GS**, Greensand Way, officially opened in 1980, is a 110 mile path from Haslemere, Surrey to Hamstreet, Kent.

Hammonds Copse, 30ha/73 acres, belongs to the Woodland Trust which welcomes walkers to wander on its paths. The conifers are being removed to convert it to traditional broad leaved wood.

Hanger is a Wessex word for a wood on a very steep slope. It may be specified as a yew or beech hanger etc.

Headley Heath is on the North Downs chalk which should not bear heath. However there are patches of clay with flints (from decay of the chalk) and gravel (dumped during the ice-age) on top of the chalk which encourage gorse, bracken and birch. The numerous flints come from all three components. The terrain was resculptured during WWII by Canadian troops practising building and destruction of airstrips and trench systems.

Holmbury Hill, 875'/261m, is part of the Hythe Sandstone ridge between Leith Hill and Pitch Hill, which are Lower Greensand promontories projecting out into the Weald. The Iron Age ramparts on top enclose an area of 8 acres/3¼ ha. The -*bury* probably derives from *burh*, Anglo Saxon for a protected enclosure.

Holmbury St Mary is a village of relatively modern origin. The contrived name is taken from the hill and the saint of the church. The parish was put together, after the church was built, from the adjacent hamlets of Abinger Sutton, Felday and Pitland Street and several London families built large houses round about after the railway was arrived. The church, St Mary, was funded and designed by the architect George Edmund Street, 1824-1881, who lived here. He was one of the greatest exponents of the Gothic revival and is best known for the Gothic law courts in The Strand. He built and restored churches and cathedrals all over Britain and one in Constantinople. Bargate is the building stone of the church and old cottages.

Holmwood is *Homewood* in old documents suggesting the name simply meant the local wood which belonged to Dorking as opposed to Iwood (now Ewood) near Newdigate or the great forest which stretched over the most of the Weald. It has numerous homesteads in it and hamlets along the turnpike road which became the A24. One of these, South Holmwood had a church from 1838, St Mary Magdalene. The Common is on the Wealden Clay.

Horsley first appears in the will of the Saxon earl, Elfrede, around 880. Part was given to the Archbishop of Canterbury in 1032 so there are two Horsleys. East Horsley is HORSLEI in the Domesday Book. It remained with the Archbishop after the Conquest for the victualling of the monks until the Dissolution.

The **Hurtwood** is the name of an area opened to the public in 1926 but stretching over several private estates and trust properties. It is mainly pine woods, forestry plantations and heath with numerous footpaths and bridleways. *Hurts* is a dialect name for bilberries and commonly found in local place-names and probably the origin of *Whortle-* and *Huckle*berry.

Jayes Park may get its name from a landowner, Joye, mentioned in 1332.

Juniper Hall is a grand 18th century country house, built on the site of a pub, the Royal Oak, and extended in Victorian times. For a short period in the 1790s it was leased as a haven for emigrés of the French Revolution. It was a Canadian Army HQ in the run up to the D-Day landings (Juno Beach) in WWII. The National Trust bought it in 1945 and leased it as a Field Studies Centre.

Leatherhead first appears in writing as Leodridan in the will of Alfred the Great, drafted around 880, as a bequest to his son Edward. In the Domesday Book it is LERET, a church with 40 acres attached to the manor of Ewell. The town has spread over the land of two Domesday Book manors on the east bank of the River Mole, TORNECROSTA (Thorncroft) and PACHESHÃ (Pachesham). Leatherhead is at the centre of Surrey and may have been the county town as the County Court was there until the 13th century. It was a market town by 1248. Mr Tylney, Queen Elizabeth's Master of the Revels, lived at the Mansion, at which time the town population would have been about 300. It was 1,087 in the 1801 census and about 21,000 in 2010. The present church, SS Mary & Nicholas, has building styles dated to around 1200 and may be on the site of a Saxon chapel of Thorncroft.

Leatherhead Bridge crosses the River Mole on 14 arches. There was a bridge here before 1362 (timber, presumably) as a patent roll of Edward III records a license to collect money for its repair. In 1782 an Act of Parliament made it the county's responsibility. Before that it was financed by tolls and endowments.

Leigh, pronounced *lye*, is a small and ancient village. The land of the parish appears to have been part of several Domesday Book manors. Formerly it was an industrial village involved in the iron smelting and working which would have deforested the neighbourhood for charcoal-making. An 8 acre iron-working site was leased in 1551. The church, St Bartholomew, though much altered in the Victorian era, has 15th century fabric but there was an earlier church as the advowsen was granted to the priory of St Mary Overy in 1202.

Leith Hill is the highest in Surrey at 294m/965 feet. The name probably comes from Anglo-Saxon *hlip*, steep. The tower is 19m/64 feet tall and takes the visitor above 1000 feet, the mythological height of a mountain in Britain. It was built in 1765 by Robert Hull of Leith Hill Place (who was later buried under the floor) and rebuilt in Gothic Baronial style by a Mr Evelyn in 1864. The land around the summit is owned by the National Trust but was originally part of Wotton Common. Visitors may climb the tower but it is not open every day.

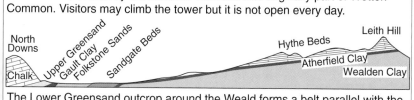

The Lower Greensand outcrop around the Weald forms a belt parallel with the North Downs but has a very irregular profile with hills only where the stratum is hard. Leith, Holmbury and Pitch Hills are a Hythe Sands escarpment, cut into a line of peaks by N-S valleys. The grey stones on the surface occur as layers of freestone in unlithified sand and were quarried for buildings. The steepness of the escarpment and valley sides is remarkable. Under the sand is the Atherfield Clay which is a division of the Lower Greensand and causes the boggy areas on the escarpment and valley bottoms. Springs on its edges undermine the sands and cut back to form the valleys. The area has low rainfall and the sand absorbs rain, so the sides are not washed down by run-off and remain steep. On the south side, slip and erosion of the clay causes occasional landslides.

The **Leith Hill Place** estate was put together by General John Foliot who lived there 1726-48. Josiah Wedgwood bought it in 1847. His wife, Caroline, created the Rhododendron Garden. She was the sister of Charles Darwin who was a frequent visitor. The composer, Ralph Vaughan-Williams, 1872-1958, a grandson of Josiah Wedgwood, inherited the estate in 1931 and bequeathed it to the National Trust in 1944.

Mickleham was the name of two manors in the Domesday Book, MICLEHAM which became Norbury Park across the Mole and MICKLEHAM whose lands straddled the Dorking-London road and became Ashurst and Box Hill. The *Running Horses* used to provide stabling for Epsom racehorses. The Church, St Michael's, is a 12th century building much re-built. The tower dates from about 1140 and the chancel arch from about 1180. The Norbury Chapel, now incorporated in the north aisle, was originally a detached 14th century chantry. There was a Domesday Book church probably on the same site.

Milton Court is a grand Jacobean house with Dutch gables built in 1611 by Richard Evelyn, father of the diarist. It is now the headquarters of Unum. The estate was the Domesday Book 6 hide manor MILDETONE. In the 13th century the manor belonged to the nuns of Kilburn Priory but became crown land after the Dissolution. In 1600 it was granted by Queen Elizabeth to George Evelyn the gunpowder magnate who already owned Wotton. The timber mill below the pond. fed by the Pipp Brook, was demolished in 1947, presumably on the site of the Domesday Book mill. The mill house remains.

The River **Mole** rises near Gatwick airport where it is culverted under the runway. It drains to the Thames, opposite Hampton Court at Molesey, from which it probably derives its present name. It was the Moulesey River in 1595. An earlier name, *Emel*, survives in Elmbridge and it was Emenan in 983. On the chalk, some of its water runs underground from several swallow holes and a 4-mile stretch can be dry above ground in summer.

The **Mole Gap** is a cleft in the North Downs through which run the River Mole, A24 and railway. It appears paradoxical that the river could cut its way through the chalk ridge but the likely explanation is that the river was there before the ridge. In the middle of the Weald about 1000m of strata have been removed. When the Chalk dome was continuous between the present N and S Downs it would have been high country with rivers down its slopes. Erosion has eaten out the middle leaving edges as ridges still traversed by rivers.

Newdigate is not mentioned in the Domesday Book which is bereft of manors in the central Weald. The population would have been scattered, eking out a living on small patches of fertile soil in the difficult terrain on Wealden Clay. The name first appears in a document of about 1165 when Hamelin, Earl of Surrey, asserted his ownership of the *Capella de Neudegat*. By 1270 this chapel is called church (*ecclesia*) in the Winchester diocesan register. The name is conjectured to derive from *On Ewood Gate*, Ewood being an ancient royal hunting estate and *gate* being an approach or way. The scattered nature of the village reflects the forest origin. The church, St Peter, has stonework in the corners of the nave predating 1200; dendrochronology indicates a felling date of 1525 for timbers in the tower. Points of interest: massive scissor bracing of the tower, east lancet windows of around 1200, dug-out church chest made from a single log, the hole in the S pier where the chained bible was anchored.

Norbury Park estate was bought by Surrey County Council in 1930 to preserve the hill as an open space of great natural beauty. Like Box Hill, it forms a corner of the North Downs where cut by the Mole Gap. Beech, oak and yew cover most of the hill; the lower slopes are farmland including Bocketts Farm. The manor house and garden on the hilltop are privately owned. The Park was developed by William Lock who bought it and built the present mansion in 1774. It is said to have inspired Fanny Burney's novel *Camilla*. Marie Stopes lived there 1938-58. The estate corresponds to the Domesday Book manor of MICLEHAM held by Oswold of Richard son of Count Gilbert. The name first appears as Le North Bury in a Chancery Inquisition of 1314.

The **NDW**, North Downs Way, a modern concoction for walkers designated in 1978 by the Countryside Commission. It runs 131 miles from Farnham to Dover mainly following ancient drove roads. Pre-historic and medieval tracks made use of ridges to avoid bogs, undergrowth and dangerous animals.

The **North Downs** are the chalk ridge along the north edge of Kent and through Surrey into Hampshire. In the Weald. the ridge is remarkably level for 100 miles, interrupted only by the rivers crossing it. This ridge is the broken edge (escarpment) of the Chalk which, rising from under the London Basin, once formed a dome over the Weald continuous with the South Downs from which the chalk dips under the English Channel to France. The steep slopes and summit clay made ploughing impossible or futile so for many centuries sheep were grazed intensively, maintaining the grassland. Pepys on a day trip to Epsum (14/7/1667).. walked upon the Downes and encountered a shepherd. He told me there was about 18 Scoare sheep in his flock, and that he hath 4s. a week...

The **Nower** near Dorking is a steep little outcrop of Hythe Sandstone (Lower Greensand). The name derives from *ōra + n* of a preceding word eg *atten*. The Anglo-Saxons had numerous distinguishing words for hills which were needed for finding the way. Fieldwork on hills of similar name suggests an *ōra* was a hill with a flat top and a convex side. Margaret Gelling & Ann Cole *Landscape of Place-names*

Ockley is HOCLEI in the Domesday Book, a manor of one hide held by Ælmer. The present village straddles a straight section of the A29 which corresponds to Stane Street. The Battle of Acled recorded in the Anglo-Saxon Chronicles for 851 is claimed for Ockley but also for Oakley near Basingstoke. This was a turning point in relations between the Saxons and the Vikings because King Ethelwulf of Wessex (father of Alfred the Great) soundly defeated the Danes.

Ockley Church, St Margaret, is ½ mile from the village. Early window styles suggest building around 1300 and 1320 but the earliest evidence of the church is in the papal taxation of 1291. The puritan rector Henry Whitfield moved to Connecticut in 1639 where his house in Guilford (sic) is the oldest in the state.

Osbrooks is a splendid 17th century house, timber framed with herringbone brickwork. Parts of it are matching 20th century extensions. There was already a house here in 1523 for there was a grant of timber for repairs that year.

Paddington is the Domesday Book PAPENDENE, a 4 hide manor in Wotton Hundred. It had a mill taxed @ 6 shillings probably on the site of the modern millhouse. The name illustrates the difficulty of interpreting the origins of place-names. The *ton* would most likely be derived from the Anglo-Saxon for farm but the name appears as PATESDON in 1215 and *don* or *dun* usually derives from the A-S for hill. The Domesday Book version has *dene* which is the A-S for valley. This is the earliest known form so is taken as the most likely origin. *Padda* was a person's name; *~ingas* meant people in an ethnic or community sense so *Surrey Place-names* interprets it as *the valley of Padda's people*.

Park House Farm, Grade II listed, has 20th century windows and tiles but at core is a 14th century 3 bay hall house with 15th and 17th century additions. One of the chimneys is 17th century. Some of the timbers date from 1364-96.

The **Pilgrims' Way** name appears to have been codified by Ordnance Survey for a trackway of prehistoric age along the dry and raised chalk lands supposedly linking Winchester and Canterbury. In Hampshire it is the Harrow Way, sometimes identified with the Tin Road from Cornwall.

Pillboxes are World War II relics of the GHQ line which stretched from the Medway to near Gloucester to defend London and the Midlands. The line follows natural obstacles such as the Downs, canals and rivers.

The **Pipp Brook** drains the eastern slopes of Leith Hill via the valley east of the Tilling. It feeds the mill ponds at the Rookery and Milton and runs through Dorking to the River Mole near Pixholme, to reach the sea via the Thames. Presumably Dorking was founded upon it as the river is off to one side.

Polesden Lacey is a National Trust property with house and grounds open to the public. Polesden first appears as a manor in 1470, a fragment cut off the Domesday Book manor of Great Bookham. The name probably derives from the Anglo-Saxon for *Poll's valley*. Anthony Rous replaced the medieval house in 1630. Sheridan, 1751-1816, the playwright, theatre manager & MP, bought it in 1804. Admiral Geary, the owner in 1884, added to the estate the manor of Polesden Lacey detached from Mickleham. The present house was built in the manner of a Grecian villa in 1824 by Thomas Cubitt for Joseph Bonsor and enlarged in the same style by Ambrose Poynter in 1906 for the Grevilles. Mrs Greville bequeathed it to the National Trust in 1942 and is buried in the garden.

Priory Park was land of Reigate Priory. The priory was founded in 1201 as a hospital of the Augustinians by William de Warenne, Earl of Surrey, and later became a house of canons. The lake derives from fish ponds which were originally more extensive. After the Dissolution, Henry VIII granted the estate to Lord William Howard, uncle of his 5th wife, in 1541. The tudor manor became the chief home of his son, High Admiral Howard of Effingham. The Georgian front was added around 1770 after a serious fire during the ownership of Richard Ireland. Randal Vogan bought the ridge in 1920 and presented it to the people of Reigate. Admiral of the Fleet Beattie bought the mansion and estate in 1921. Subsequently the mansion has been a business HQ and school. The mansion and estate were bought by the borough in 1947.

The **railway** line, east-west along the North Downs, was built by the RGRR (Reading, Guildford & Reigate Railway) Company and opened in 1849 making use of a new tunnel of the L&SWR to pass under the Downs at Guildford.

The **railway** line, north-south through the Mole Gap, Holmwood and Ockley, opened from Epsom-Leatherhead 1/2/1859 bringing London trains to Dorking 11/3/1867 and Horsham 1/5/1867. It was an extension of the LBSCR (London to Brighton and South Coast Railway) line which opened to Epsom 10/5/1847.

Ranmore Common is a belt of woodland on clay-with-flints overlying the chalk along the southern edge of the old manor of Great Bookham. *Ran* was Anglo-Saxon for boundary strip but the first documentary appearance of the name is in Bowen's *Map of the County of Surrey* of 1749. The army camped on the common in 1780 at the time of the Gordon Riots. The Pilgrims' Way or Harow Way and North Downs Way run along the southern edge.

Ranmore Church, St Barnabas, is a Gothic Revival church built in 1859 for George Cubitt (1st Baron Ashdown), son of the London builder. Its position and sharp spire makes it a distinctive landmark from many places in this book.

Reigate Stone is a calcareous sandstone forming a 10ft seam in the Upper Greensand which outcrops beneath the Chalk at the foot of the North Downs escarpment. It was mined with adits between Buckland and Godstone until the 20th century. It is recorded in use for the Palace of Whitehall in 1259 and was considered for the Houses of Parliament. It is equivalent to the clunch of East Anglia and the malmstone of Hampshire.

Reigate was a hundred as well as a manor in the Domesday Book but was then called CHERCHEFELLE. The name *Reigata* first appears in a deed of around 1170 and it was called a borough in assize records of 1291. William the Conqueror awarded the manor to William de Warenne who became the first Earl of Surrey in 1088. The town appears to have grown around the medieval castle or the priory. It became a municipal borough in 1863. The first Surrey turnpike was the Crawley to Reigate road in 1696. Redhill arose as a Victorian new town in the parish when the London-Brighton railway line arrived.

The **Rice Bridge** is first documented as the farm *Risbrig* in a fine of 1198. The name derives from a pile of brushwood serving as a causeway across water. There may have been a temporary crossing of the Mole in summer or of a stream somewhere else on the farm but it could have arrived as a surname.

The **Rookery** is a cluster of houses built on the land of a country house of that name, the birth place and early home of Thomas Malthus, Cambridge mathematician, curate of Okewood and FRS. His *Essay on the Principles of Population* was a seminal contribution to human ecology which influenced Darwin, Keynes and Marx. Senex's map of 1729 shows two Pipp Brook mills.

Shellwood is not a Domesday Book manor but was evidently an outlying property of the royal manor of Ewell. Shellwood first comes to light in 1158 when part of the lands of Ewell was granted to Merton Priory by Henry II. After the Dissolution of the Monasteries it was hived off as a separate estate.

Sheepleas was bought from the West Horsley estate in the 1930s to be a Protected Open Space. On the north face of the Downs, it is a patchwork of woodland and chalk grassland of 108 ha/267 acres with a rich flora and an abundance of Roman snails. In place names ~*ley*, ~*lea* and ~*leigh* usually derive from the Anglo Saxon *leah*, clearing, so it is probable the grass patches were used for or even caused by sheep grazing.

Stane Street was the Roman road direct from London Bridge to Noviomagus Reginorum, Chichester, not straight but with deflections to avoid Leith Hill and Box Hill. It was built soon after the Conquest. The paved width was 7.4m/54 Roman feet. The outer ditches were 25.6m apart. Most of it is under existing roads or tracks. *Stane* derives from *stone*.

The **stepping stones** at the foot of Box Hill are at the position of a River Mole ford. The earliest reference to them is in 1842. They were removed for WWII and dedicated anew in 1946 by PM Atlee. The flat area below the stepped path is the Weypole, apparently taking its name from a post marking the ford.

The **Tillingbourne** is a major tributary of the River Wey. It runs 20 km/13 miles between the Greensand and chalk ridges fed by springs from both and joins the Wey near Shalford waterworks. It powered up to 30 mills and was a major industrial valley of England until the Industrial Revolution. Now it sustains trout farms and watercress beds. Derived from Anglo-Saxon, *bourn* and *burn* mean brook or stream so *Tillingbourne Stream* is tautological.

The **trig points** passed on walks in this book are pillars in concrete or local stone. They were constructed in the 1940s for the third triangulation of Great Britain which had been initiated in 1936. Leith Hill Tower was used as a trig point in 1938 when the primary network of trig points was set up across the country using sightings of up to 50 km/30 miles.

Westcott is one of the chain of villages along the Lower Greensand outcrop on the south edge of the North Downs probably originally settled on streams from chalk springs overflowing the gault clay. The land was the large manor of WESCOTE in the Domesday Book. The Evelyn family added it to their land-holdings of the adjacent Wotton and Milton. The church, Holy Trinity, was built by Sir Gilbert Scott in 14th century style and consecrated in 1852.

Westhumble appears first as Wysthumble in an Assize Roll of 1248 but could well be the village of the Domesday Book manor of MICLEHAM which became the Norbury estate. The early village appears to have been east of the present centre under the 1940s housing estate, near the ancient high road through the Mole gap. The little church is unusual as being labelled chapel of ease. Fanny Burney, the Georgian novelist, had a house in the village with her husband the French General Alexandre D'Arbley who had been an emigré at Juniper Hall.

Elmer's **Windmill** above Ockley was restored as a residence in 2010 using the 21 foot brick base of the working mill which had fallen out of use around 1912 and disintegrated in 1944. It was built in 1803 for £735 5s 9¼d on a site where there is no evidence of any earlier mill. Being cloaked in horizontal planks it is octagonal which makes it a smock mill. It gets its name from the farm which presumably gets its name from Ælmer the pre-Conquest Saxon owner of Ockley manor recorded by the Domesday Book, 1086.

Reigate Heath **Windmill** is a post mill. The working mechanism was attached to a single post which could be rotated to suit the wind direction - in this case by hand using a tail pole. It is said to have been erected in 1765 but there was a mill here in Bowen's map of Surrey 1753. Milling ceased in 1862. It became a chapel of ease to St Mary's Church Reigate in 1880. The roundhouse enclosing the base of the post is St Cross Chapel for a congregation of 50.

Wonham Mill ceased milling in 1930 and was disused for many years until converted into apartments in 2011. Wonham is first heard of in 1199 when a William de Wonham received a grant of Betchworth land which became a separate manor so the mill is probably on the site of the Domesday Book mill of Betchworth. Edward III's confirmation of land ownership by Reigate Priory in 1328 included the water mill at Wonham. The millhouse is 18th century. The name may derive from Anglo-Saxon *wõgan hamme*, crooked river bank.

Wotton parish, probably corresponding to the Saxon estate, is 6 miles long N-S but only one mile wide. H E Malden postulated Wotten was a boundary of the Saxons before they pushed eastwards through Surrey. He suggests the name derives from Woden who was the god of boundaries. West of Wotton is a cluster of pre-Christian Anglo Saxon place-names. In the Domesday Book WODETON is a Surrey hundred with the manor written as ODETONE on the next line. John Evelyn, the diarist grew up here and in later years inherited it from his elder brother. The estate had been bought in 1579 by his grandfather, George Evelyn, 1530-1603, who was the first mass producer of gunpowder in England using local mills. The family have owned it ever since, adding Abinger, Westcott and Milton manors. The church, St John the Evangelist, appears to have walls pre-dating the Conquest. It has elaborate memorials of the Evelyns.

Wotton House is now a hotel and conference centre. It is the manor house and the seat of the Evelyn family. The splendid Tudor front is actually Victorian.